God, Where Are You?

Suffering and Faith

Kaleidoscope

Statement of Purpose

Kaleidoscope is a series of adult educational resources developed for the ecumenical church by Lancaster Theological Seminary and the United Church Board for Homeland Ministries. Developed for adults who want serious study and dialogue on contemporary issues of Christian faith and life, Kaleidoscope offers elective resources designed to provide new knowledge and new understanding for persons who seek personal growth and a deeper sense of social responsibility in their lives.

Kaleidoscope utilizes the expertise of professionals in various disciplines to develop study resources in both print and video. The series also provides tools to help persons develop skills in studying, reflecting, inquiring critically, and exploring avenues of appropriate Christian responses in life.

Kaleidoscope provides sound and tested resources in theology, biblical studies, ethics, and other related subjects that link personal growth and social responsibility to life situations in which adult Christian persons develop.

God, Where Are You?

Suffering and Faith

Richard F. Vieth

A Kaleidoscope Series Resource

United Church Press
New York

To Scott and Mark:
sons that make a father proud.

KALEIDOSCOPE SERIES

Library of Congress Cataloging-in-Publication Data

Vieth, Richard F., 1927–
  God, where are you?

  (A Kaleidoscope series resource)
  Bibliography: p. 93
  1. Suffering—Religious aspects—Christianity.
2. Theodicy. I. Title. II. Series.
BT732.7.V497   1989   231'.8   89-5007
ISBN 0-8298-0816-7
ISBN 0-8298-0817-5 (Leader's guide ed.)

United Church Press, 475 Riverside Drive, New York, NY 10115

Contents

Introduction to the Kaleidoscope Series

Through direct experience, our faculty at Lancaster Theological Seminary discovered that a continual demand exists for Christian theological reflection upon issues of current interest. To meet this demand, the Seminary for many years has offered courses for lay people. To offer the substance of these courses to the wider Christian public is the purpose of the Kaleidoscope Series.

Lancaster Seminary exists to proclaim the gospel of Jesus Christ for the sake of the church and the world. In addition to preparing men and women for the ordained Christian ministry, the Seminary seeks to be a center of theological reflection for clergy and laity. Continuing education and leadership development for all Christians focus our mission. The topics and educational style in the Kaleidoscope Series extend Lancaster Seminary's commitment: theological study reflective of the interaction of the Bible, the world, the church, worship, and personal faith. We hope that this course will provide an opportunity for you to grow in self-understanding, in knowledge of other people and God's creation, and in the spirit of Christ.

We wish to thank the staff of the Division of Education and Publication of the United Church Board for Homeland Ministries for their leadership in this enterprise. The Rev. Dr. Ansley Coe Throckmorton, The Rev. Dr. Larry E. Kalp, and The Rev. Dr. Percel O. Alston provided encouragement and support for the project. In particular, we are grateful for the inspiration of Percel Alston, who was a trustee of Lancaster Seminary. His life-long interest in adult education makes it most appropriate that this series be dedicated to him. Three other staff members have guided the series through the writing and production stages: The Rev. Jack H. Haney, Project Coordinator for the Kaleidoscope Series, The Rev. Nancy G. Wright, Editor for Kaleidoscope, and Mr. Gene Permé, Marketing Director. As a publishing staff they have provided valuable experience and counsel. Finally, I wish to recognize the creative leadership of Mrs. Jean Vieth, the Seminary Coordinator for the Series, who has been active for several years in this educational program at Lancaster.

Peter M. Schmiechen, President
The Lancaster Theological Seminary

Chapter 1

Hurting and Wholeness

Suffering: all of us know what it is, because all have suffered. Life inescapably involves suffering, to a greater or lesser extent. It is universal.

Yet suffering is also unique. What it means to the person afflicted depends on his or her temperament, prior experiences, and upbringing, including religious orientation. The only way to find out what suffering means is to ask the afflicted person and to listen carefully to what he or she has to tell.

Even so, there are things that characterize our common human experiences of suffering. These are worth examining so that we can better understand our own afflictions and help others cope with theirs. Let us begin with the very concept of suffering.

Most of us are fairly concrete thinkers. When we hear an abstract term like *suffering*, we associate with it some concrete picture that represents for us the meaning of the word. What is the picture that comes to mind when you hear the word *suffering*? Perhaps you envision someone racked by cancer, afflicted with a migraine, or tormented by a painful injury. Perhaps you picture a marriage torn by divorce or a family lacerated by grief. The list of possible examples is limitless, but to see suffering more concretely, let us look at one person's suffering in greater detail. Here is part of a letter from a father (let's call him Carl), written on the day of his son's funeral:

> It really hurt. I could feel the pain stabbing right into my chest as they began lowering my firstborn into the grave beneath the green hills that had given him so much pleasure. Suddenly I was overcome by the emotions I had struggled to control all during the funeral, and tears blurred my vision.
>
> As I resisted letting go of Bill's life, pictures crowded into my mind: Carolyn beaming as she cradled him in her arms the day he was born; the three of us building sand castles together on the beach; his triumphant

1

expression when he took first prize in the high school essay contest; the day we took him off to college.

Many of the more vivid images were not so pleasant: his body racked with nausea at the beginning of each chemotherapy treatment; the shock of first seeing his bald head and bleeding gums; the wincing pain on his face each time the needle was inserted into his bone marrow; the hope draining from his eyes (and mine) each time the doctor gave him bad news.

What hurt even more were the pictures of things Bill would never have a chance to experience: receiving his sheepskin at college commencement (he missed it by only three weeks!); beginning a career and taking pride in new achievements; falling in love and getting married; holding his firstborn, as I had held him. . . . Are these tears for Bill or for myself?

I suppose it's perverse, but one thing I feel good about. When I buried him, I buried that damned cancer! The cells that killed my son will never afflict anyone else.

Using this letter and the other examples of suffering listed above—migraines, injury, divorce, bereavement—what is the common characteristic that makes us regard them all as instances of suffering? Wherein lies the *sufferingness?* The most obvious common thread is that all are *painful.* "It really *hurt,*" says the bereaved father, who goes on to describe the pain and locate it anatomically. Indeed, all the afflictions in our short list can be experienced in connection to a specific part of the body: head, chest, limb, or organ. Even the suffering in divorce and bereavement, which does not derive from bodily injury, is expressed in physical images of tearing and laceration.

It would appear, then, that suffering is a form of pain or is so closely analogous to it that we can use physical pain as a model for understanding what human suffering is all about. Pain, we all know from personal experience, is an unpleasant physical sensation, an ache or discomfort that has a specific bodily location. *Webster's New World Dictionary* defines pain as "a sensation of hurting, or strong discomfort, in some part of the body, caused by an injury, disease, or functional disorder, and transmitted through the nervous system." This is followed by a further definition of pain as "the distress or *suffering,* mental or physical, caused by great anxiety, anguish, grief, disappointment, etc."[1] Here suffering is listed as a species of pain, and this is further supported by *Random House Dictionary's* definition of suffering: "to undergo or feel pain or distress."[2] This interpretation seems to be supported by common use, for *pain* is the word we most frequently associate with suffering.

Certainly a close relationship exists between pain and suffering, for physical and mental distress is the constant companion of suffering.

Yet several common experiences should make us hesitate to equate the two. Childbirth, for instance, can be an excruciatingly painful event. The *New World Dictionary*, in fact, lists "the labor of childbirth" as its fourth meaning for the word *pain*. Yet we would scarcely consider childbirth prototypical of suffering. Labor pains are a temporary side effect of a joyous event, which many would regard as the very antithesis of suffering. At most one might say, "She's suffering right now, but . . ." Suffering implies something long-term and something threatening to a person's future. At the point at which giving birth endangers the mother's life, pain becomes suffering.

Similarly, the aches and pains that athletes endure are notorious, but we do not cite them as paradigms of suffering. In fact, athletes sometimes become so caught up in their sport that they fail to notice the pain until the event is over. Musicians, dancers, and other artists report similar experiences. When a crippling injury places an athlete's or artist's future in jeopardy, however, pain signals suffering.

Michelle

The distinction between pain and suffering becomes more than a word game when we turn to the field of medicine. Just how dangerous it can be for physicians to interpret suffering on the model of pain is explained by Eric J. Cassell, M.D., of the Harvard Medical School.[3] Interpreting suffering as physiological pain, he argues, can lead the physician to follow a course of treatment that actually adds to the patient's suffering instead of relieving it.

To illustrate this idea, Cassell cites the case of a thirty-five-year-old sculptor with breast cancer. Cassell does not identify her, but for convenience, let us call her Michelle. Although Cassell describes her physicians as caring as well as competent, he states that Michelle was unable to get from them adequate and honest information about her condition and treatment. That left her terrified in the face of a threatening future: fearful of the pain and loss tomorrow might bring and sure that she would soon die. In the course of treatment, her ovaries were removed to slow the spread of cancer. When a tumor sapped the strength from her sculpting hand, she became profoundly depressed. She also feared losing her friends because of the changes in her appearance—including weight gain—and life-style that therapy produced. "We know why that young woman suffered," Cassell states. "She was housebound and bedbound, her face was changed by steroids, she was masculinized by her treatment, one breast was scarred, and she had almost no hair."[4] While Michelle also had severe pain, which her physicians treated, she suffered much more from the terrifying threats to her personal, professional, and social future, to which they did not attend.

For Cassell the case illustrates medicine's preoccupation with the physical body and physical illness. This is based on the now-outmoded dualism of body and mind traceable back to the seventeenth century philosopher René Descartes. Traditionally, medical professionals, Cassell claims, have tended to consider suffering either as physical pain (lumping "pain and suffering" together in a single phrase) or else as something "mental" and therefore outside their realm—perhaps even imaginary. Michelle's physicians regarded her suffering as pain brought on by a malignant tumor, and they treated the malignancy and pain with the best means at their disposal. Her fears of isolation and impending doom were left for Michelle to cope with on her own.

From the case Cassell draws three major points. First, it is persons who suffer, not bodies or minds. Second, suffering may be defined as a state of personal distress arising when impending destruction of the person is perceived. Third, persons are multifaceted, and suffering can occur in any facet of personal existence. Let us examine each of Cassell's points in greater detail.

1. Persons, not bodies, suffer

It is persons who suffer. To lodge suffering in either the body or the mind is a major category mistake, for suffering belongs in the domain of personal language. It was Michelle who was suffering, not her breast. For this reason, treating a human malady in the same way that a mechanic would repair a malfunctioning auto part increases the patient's suffering instead of alleviating it. A major cause of misunderstanding between patients and physicians, Cassell alleges, is a fundamental difference in perception of the goals of medicine. Patients expect physicians to be concerned with relief of suffering, whatever its source. Physicians, on the other hand, have traditionally limited their attention to the body and its diseases. If relief of suffering is to be the goal of medicine, then the only adequate approach will be one that listens attentively to the patient's account of her or his suffering and includes this in the treatment.

2. Suffering threatens wholeness

Suffering is the state of severe distress occurring when a person confronts impending destruction or disintegration.[5] A number of important aspects of this definition need to be highlighted. First, what is threatened is, in Cassell's words, a person's "intactness" or "wholeness" or "integrity."

Thus the apparent danger may be to the person's life, or it may be to some aspect of that life perceived as essential to its meaning. For Michelle, both her life and significant aspects of it were endangered. By contrast, Carl's life (the grieving father) was not in danger, but a huge piece of the meaning of his life had been dislodged forever with the death of his son.

Second, this definition holds the subjective and the objective together: suffering is an inner distress resonating to an external threat. It is virtually a reflex response to impending danger, something persons "undergo" or "endure" (as the dictionaries put it), rather than something the sufferer initiates. In this sense suffering is *passive*. At the same time, the afflicted person's way of coping will greatly affect the quality of suffering and the speed of recovery. Hence "*active* suffering*" is a useful notion. Part of Cassell's criticism of Michelle's treatment is that her physicians kept her role passive rather than involving her in her therapy.

Third, *distress*—coming from the Latin *distringere*, "to stretch out, to pull apart"—is an appropriate word to describe this inner state, for the sufferer is "strung out" to the point of "coming apart" and must struggle to hold life together. Distress conjures up images of emotional turmoil, the strong feelings we expect to accompany suffering, especially in its early stages. Cassell lists sadness, anger, loneliness, depression, grief, unhappiness, melancholy, rage, withdrawal, and yearning as some of the feelings commonly associated with suffering. We know that it is important to find avenues of expression for these feelings. Sharing them with others hastens the healing process, while bottling them up can impede recovery. In our culture it is men in particular who, by their upbringing, are inclined to suppress feelings and avoid sharing them with others. Important as the psychological aspect of suffering is, we need to remember that distress includes physical as well as mental strain. Body and mind constitute a single whole, and suffering will have somatic as well as emotional impact.

Fourth, the phrase "*impending* destruction" shows that suffering has a future orientation. The sufferer fears that he or she will be destroyed imminently, or will come apart, or won't be able to get life back together. Carl, the bereaved father, is suffering from the loss of a piece of himself central to his life's meaning, and he must wonder if the void left by his son's death can ever be filled. Michelle's fears of the future all but overwhelm her. Such suffering will end, Cassell tells us, only when the impending threat has passed or when the sufferer finds some other way to rebuild wholeness. Carl will have to take the latter route, fashioning a life that is meaningful despite the loss of his son.

What possibilities Michelle has for overcoming suffering are not clear from the data Cassell gives us.

In the final analysis, suffering is unique to each person. Cassell notes that suffering occurs when impending danger is perceived *by the person threatened,* not by an outside observer. Michelle's physicians are well aware of the danger cancer poses to their patient, but they apparently have not perceived the way she is threatened by the prescribed treatment. Sometimes it is the other way around: what the outside observer perceives as a menacing danger is viewed as a challenge by the one threatened. As the old proverb has it: "One person's meat is another's poison." Even when sufferer and observer perceive the same threat, the outsider still will not know what the threat means to the sufferer. This will depend on the person's temperament, prior history, orientation toward life, and so on. A man who has a heart attack at the same age as his father's fatal attack may figure "This is it." A woman who views her life as a series of failures is likely to approach life-threatening illness as one more failure. By contrast, editor and author Norman Cousins (*Anatomy of an Illness as Perceived by the Patient*) attacked his cancer aggressively and resolved not to be defeated by it. Because each person is unique, only the person suffering can say what that suffering means. In the field of medicine, Cassell is telling us that an objective diagnosis may inform us what the disease is but cannot tell us what the suffering is. The patient alone can do that; hence it is essential that physician, pastor, or friend listen carefully to the afflicted person's assessment of his or her suffering. This is the reason that it is always a mistake to think, "I know exactly what you're going through," and why this remark is often met by anger. Instead of listening to the hurting person, the friend who says this is probably attending to his or her own feelings and experience.

A further consequence of personal uniqueness is that there are limits to the generalizations that can be made about human suffering. Two decades ago Elisabeth Kübler-Ross made history with the publication of *On Death and Dying,* which traced a sequence of five stages in the dying process: denial, anger, bargaining, depression, and acceptance.[6] Pastors and counselors found Kübler-Ross's construct enormously helpful, but as they began putting it to use, they also discovered its limitations. Some persons skipped stages, some proceeded through them in a different order. Many were in more than one stage at a given time, or cycled back to an earlier stage, or never reached the final stage of acceptance. Furthermore, how persons experienced each stage and coped with its challenges were different with each individual. Thus, although it is useful to know stages of dying or grief or affliction, we must beware of imposing them on others. It is not helpful to try to push a person out of denial or into acceptance, and it is not healthy for a suffering person to think, "What am I supposed to be feeling now?" Consequently, important as conceptual understanding is, no amount of book learning can substitute for actually listening to the suffering person's own understanding of what is happening to her or him.

3. Persons are multifaceted

Because persons are complex, multifaceted beings, suffering can occur in any aspect of personal existence. A person is not just a mind or a body or a spirit, but all these and more. Cassell offers "a simplified description of the person," which includes his or her relation with self, body, family, social group, role in society, transcendent source of meaning, and a great deal more. Even though suffering may arise or focus in one such facet of personal existence, it should be obvious that the suffering will affect other areas of the person's life. Carl's mental anguish, precipitated by a family loss, manifested itself in bodily pain. Michelle's suffering arose in her body but profoundly affected every other facet of her existence.

The Causes of Suffering

So far we have attended to the subjective side of suffering. Looking now at the objective causes of suffering, we will examine the kinds of external dangers that threaten a person with destruction or disintegration. Already we have considered two common sources of suffering, disease and death. To that we could add tornado, flood, war, crime, torture, hunger, eviction, unemployment, divorce—the list is virtually endless. Cassell clusters these causes of suffering under three broad categories: pain, injury, and loss. Most dictionary definitions list the same three.[7] Other categories sometimes listed, such as harm or grief, can be included under injury or loss. I propose adding a fourth category that does not fit well under any of the other three, namely, oppression. We will examine these four briefly to see what the suffering is that corresponds to each. We must remind ourselves that because suffering is unique to each person, the most we can claim is that these four are potential threats to the wholeness of any person.

1. Pain

We have scrupulously discriminated between suffering and pain, so why bring pain back into the picture? The answer is that sometimes pain itself threatens to destroy or shatter a person. Consider what pain meant to Michelle. First of all, it signified cancer, and for her that was the sentence of impending death. Furthermore, the recurrence of pain signaled further disability, disfigurement, and isolation, with no end in sight. Cassell describes several situations in which a person suffers as a result of his or her reading of what pain means:

> "If the pain continues like this, I *will be* overwhelmed"; "If the pain comes from cancer, I *will* die"; "If the pain cannot be controlled, I *will not* be able to take it."[8]

Based on such situations, Cassell lists four kinds of pain that have the potential to produce suffering: pain that is *overwhelming, uncontrollable, chronic,* or that *signals a dire consequence.* Once again (as Cassell's italics show), it is fear of a disastrous future that precipitates suffering. Wherever dread of the future can be dispelled, suffering from the pain will abate. Specifically, if overwhelming pain can be reduced to manageable proportions, if intractable pain can be brought under control, if there is hope for an end to chronic pain, if a dreaded diagnosis is disconfirmed, then suffering from the pain itself will diminish or disappear.

2. Injury

Auto accidents are a major source of injury today. All of us have known persons who have been seriously disfigured in such an accident. Even where no continuing disability or chronic pain accompanies the deformity, the damage to the person's self-image and self-worth remains. Often such persons are ashamed to show themselves in public, afraid of how others may respond.

I have a childhood friend who lost his right hand in a freak accident. I was amazed at how quickly he recovered and how versatile he was with only one hand. He was more adept at sports than I was with two hands! Yet I noticed that when not engaged in activity, he kept that right stub concealed in his pocket, a clear indication of shame. In adulthood he was never able to hold a job for very long, even though he was a handsome and intelligent young man. Eventually, he settled into becoming a househusband, while his wife worked full time.

An even more extreme example is Michelle. A scarred breast, obesity, a masculinized appearance, and loss of hair severely damaged the self-image of this artistic young woman, leading her to fear that former friends would no longer want to see her. "Disease," says Cassell, "can so alter the relation [of a person to his or her own body] that the body is no longer seen as a friend but, rather, as an untrustworthy enemy."[9] Michelle's case also shows us how much a person's self-image and self-worth are shaped by cultural values and expectations, and how the social context can either exaggerate or mitigate personal affliction.

Domestic violence, which has only recently surfaced in the public's awareness, further illustrates the way injury induces suffering. Abused children and spouses tend to blame themselves for the problem, resulting in shame and low self-esteem. They feel tainted, like damaged goods. This, combined with the distorted image of intimacy in an abusive family, makes it difficult for those who have been abused to establish meaningful relationships. Personal integrity has been violated, and the abused find it difficult to believe that they can ever become whole persons again.

3. Loss

Loss is a category that overlaps injury, because many injuries result in losses. These can be physical, mental, emotional, or social losses. Loss is a much larger category than injury, for life is, among other things, a series of losses, brought on by the life cycle, social mobility, professional advancement, and life's inevitable tragedies, great and small. The new adventures that give zest to human existence are bittersweet, always involving good-byes as well as hellos. Some losses are so familiar that they need not be detailed: loss of relationships, limbs, sight or sound, abilities, employment, income, home, reputation. Because such losses are severely threatening to personal wholeness, they can provoke profound suffering.

Another common experience is loss of objects, but, like so many other aspects of suffering, it is not so much the object itself as the meaning associated with it that is important. Several years ago a move made it necessary for me to sell my trailer and model railroad. Neither of these items had been used for years, and my wife (who did the dirty deed for me) got a good price for them. What made the loss difficult for me (and still brings a tear to my eye as I write this) was that I had built both of them with my own hands, and the family had enjoyed using both of them for many years. It was difficult to bid farewell to that piece of myself.

More significant was the complaint made by a pastor concerning a parishioner who had recently moved into one room in a retirement center. The parishioner, he said, was constantly lamenting the fact that she wasn't permitted to bring her piano and her collection of Hummel figurines. The pastor chided her for her "materialism," completely missing the real significance of these items for her.

Cassell reports an even more subtle loss, one that would likely go unnoticed by anyone save the sufferer. "Everyone has a secret life," he observes, including fantasies, love affairs, hopes, and above all, dreams. When age, illness, or injury takes away a person's secret life, the distress can be quite acute, because it must be suffered privately.

Several years ago my ninety-one-year-old mother moved into a nursing home. She was delighted with the move because she was no longer able to fend for herself in her cottage. At that point she had already lost her husband, one of her children, her two sisters and brother, her hearing, and the home in which she had lived most of her life. Since the move, physical and mental disabilities have forced her to give up most of the activities that once gave her pleasure: walking, writing, reading, and visiting friends. One thing seems to keep her going. For the past year, each time I have visited her she has said to me, "I'm going to visit my mother in Missouri next Sunday—will you take me to the airport?" Of course her health would never permit her to make the thousand-mile trip, but, more important, her mother has been dead for thirty years. My efforts to bring her to reality merely produced a dour expression and a change of subject. I soon learned that I was taking away her one remaining dream. Now I simply reply, "Of course, Mother; I'll take you to the airport whenever you're ready," knowing that that time will never come.

A crucial aspect of every person's life is what Cassell calls "the transcendent dimension," by which he means the bigger-than-me reality that is the source, ground, and goal of life. Cassell claims that every person has some transcendent dimension that gives life its wholeness and meaning. For most of us that reality is God. The significance of this transcendent dimension for healing has been too long ignored by the medical profession, he claims. Given this importance, loss of the transcendent dimension will likely be a very distressing experience for any person.

Elie Wiesel, raised in Hungary in his beloved tradition of Hasidic Judaism, experienced the loss of the sacred when he was transported to Auschwitz at the age of fourteen. On his first night in the death camp he was separated from his mother and sister and marched past huge, flaming ditches filled with babies being cremated.

> Never shall I forget that night, the first night in camp, which has turned my life into one long night, seven times cursed and seven times sealed. Never shall I forget that smoke. Never shall I forget the little faces of the children, whose bodies I saw turned into wreaths of smoke beneath a silent blue sky.
>
> Never shall I forget those flames which consumed my faith forever.
>
> Never shall I forget that nocturnal silence which deprived me, for all

eternity, of the desire to live. Never shall I forget those moments which murdered my God and my soul and turned my dreams to dust. [10]

It might be said that Wiesel's life ever since has been a struggle to rebuild faith.

Wiesel is an extreme example of persons who have lost the transcendent dimension, but we have all known persons whose faith has been shaken or broken by tragedy. I recall a parishioner who, having lost both parents under particularly cruel circumstances, was never again able to worship the loving God of her childhood. Rabbi Harold Kushner wrote *When Bad Things Happen to Good People* out of his effort to rebuild a viable faith when his earlier beliefs were shattered by the death of his son. [11] Suffering's challenge to faith, expressed in the familiar "Why?" and echoed in Jesus' own cry from the cross, "My God, my God, why have you forsaken me?" will occupy our attention throughout much of this study.

4. Oppression

Most of the pain, injury, and loss we have been considering—with the exception of that suffered by Elie Wiesel—produce the afflictions that many North Americans have in mind when they think of suffering. These afflictions strike people in situations of relative prosperity, adequate health care, and political freedom. We might speak of this as "First World" suffering; these are the afflictions of the middle and upper classes in Europe, North America, and Japan.

For the majority of the world's population (and for some people in North America) however, there is another whole layer of suffering that comes from poverty, subjugation, and poor health care. Such awareness as we have of this level of suffering comes to us mainly through the news media. A few years ago we were shocked to see the fly-covered faces of thousands of children bloated from starvation in the African Sahel. We heard incredible stories of genocide in the "killing fields" of Cambodia. We read about the murder of tens of thousands by death squads in El Salvador. We learned of a worldwide epidemic of torture practiced by most countries of the world, including the U.S. Central Intelligence Agency. [12] We watched the news reports of flooding in Bangladesh, which left thirty million homeless, one hundred thousand afflicted by diarrhea (the world's leading cause of death among children), and thousands dead. And these are but a few of the more eye-catching headline stories of recent years.

These forms of suffering most of us have never experienced or even witnessed. We can scarcely imagine what it would mean to undergo such ordeals. Yet dire living conditions are simply facts of life for the billions of people in what is called the Third World: the underdeveloped countries of our planet, largely concentrated in Africa, Asia, and South America.

Filipino Methodist Priscilla Padolina has assembled a collage of Third World suffering:

—a landless tenant exploited by the landlord;
—tribal minorities pushed to the fringes of the country;
—the factory worker whose wages will not buy enough food;
—a woman who has to sell her body to survive;
—a political prisoner who is subjected to torture;
—women in captivity because they have to walk long miles for water;
—children brought up in the slums with no hope for the future;
—illiterate masses kept in the dark;
—blacks under apartheid systems;
—untouchables and unrecognized outcasts.

It is to such persons, Padolina reminds us, that Jesus proclaimed his gospel of "good news to the poor" (Luke 4:18; cf. 6:20).[13]

We should not forget to include among the world's poor the homeless, the rural poor, and those stifled in the ghettos of our own country. Over the past two decades a process has been taking place that is sometimes referred to as "the third-worldization of the U.S." The unemployed and working poor slip ever deeper into poverty, and the gap between rich and poor ever widens. The suffering of this segment of our country's population is also foreign to the experience of most North Americans.

It is difficult to find a word that encompasses the broad range of suffering just described, but the one that seems to capture it best is *oppression*. It comes from the Latin *opprimere*, which means "to press upon, press down; to crush, smother, stamp out."[14] It conjures up a vivid image: people at the bottom of the heap, laboring under the weight of all the social strata that benefit from their employment (or unemployment). These are the powerless, pushed out of the mainstream of society and locked out of the halls of decision making. These are the people crushed or even stamped out by social forces that deny their right to exist. Oppression may consist of economic deprivation or exploitation, political powerlessness or tyrannization, social marginalization or persecution. It may result from the cruel policies of a social elite, as in the Union of South Africa; or from societal indifference to existing injustices, as in the United States; or perhaps just from lack of local leverage to change economic realities. The consequences for the oppressed are the same. More insidious than any of these factors are the justifying ideologies that penetrate the minds of the victims with the message that their suffering is God's will, or immutable fate, or their own fault.

We must remember, of course, that this entire layer of suffering comes on top of the afflictions that all humans endure. Oppressed people experience the same pain, injury, and loss as their more affluent sisters and brothers, but these are in addition to their poverty and powerlessness. Furthermore, their suffering from common human afflictions is intensified by their plight. Life expectancy is shorter, and infant mortality is high. The sight of a small casket in a funeral procession is an everyday picture in the Third World. Minor diseases and natural disasters take a much higher toll. Medical treatment is more scarce and frequently more expensive than, say, in the United States. When a volunteer worker among Salvadoran refugees in Honduras was herself stricken by cancer, she observed that she would get much better treatment in the United States than refugees with the same disease could ever expect to receive in Honduras.

The limitations of this study will not permit us to give a great deal of attention to oppression. Our focus will be on those kinds of suffering that people in U.S. churches commonly face. It is important, however, that we hold oppression before us as a widespread type of human suffering. Not only do many of our brothers and sisters on spaceship Earth suffer from oppression, but, if truth be told, most of us in the United States are unwitting conspirators in oppression. The relatively low prices of our clothing and cars, for instance, are made possible by the sweatshops of Asia, where laborers eke out a meager living under conditions that would be illegal in the United States. Even many of the toys we give our children at Christmastime are made possible by the exploitation of poor people elsewhere in the world. We need to keep this global perspective as we examine kinds of suffering that are closer to home.

In summary, suffering is the condition of severe distress that arises when a person perceives his or her wholeness to be imperiled by pain, injury, loss, or oppression. Eric Cassell has helped us to see how important *meaning* is in all this.

In the next three chapters we will examine the "why" question that arises when transcendent meaning is undermined or destroyed. In chapter 5 we will explore the way in which the story of Christ's suffering gives meaning to our stories of suffering. In the final chapter of this book we will identify resources for recovering wholeness, especially the resource of religious faith, or the transcendent dimension, which Cassell calls "probably the most powerful way in which one is restored to wholeness."[15]

Chapter 2

Where Was God Tuesday Morning?

In the first chapter we defined suffering as "the state of severe distress occurring when a person confronts impending destruction or disintegration." We discovered that both the perception of the threat and the mode of coping are unique to the sufferer, so that no one can truly claim to know what another is going through without listening carefully to that person's story. At the same time, we observed that there are some characteristics of suffering sufficiently general to be worth knowing. More of these will surface as we proceed with our study. The chapter concluded with a classification of the sources of suffering under the categories of pain, injury, loss, and oppression.

This chapter begins with a specific case—a true story with names disguised—which will enable us to apply our learnings and develop them further, and which will introduce the "why" question. No one story could be representative of human suffering, but the following case illustrates some common features and raises key issues.

Murder on the Highway

Pastor Frederick Werner hung up the phone, shaking his head in disbelief. Gayle murdered on the highway? Gayle Frey-Turner, that independent, free spirit flying in the wind? Gayle, who brought joy to all around her? *Murdered?* How could it be?

Details of the brutal slaying two hundred miles away were few and fuzzy. Apparently Gayle, having run out of gas on the interstate en route home from her night job at San Diego Naval Base, had been shot to death in her car beside the highway by an unknown assailant about 1:30 A.M. Tuesday. Perhaps her parents could tell him more when he got to their house.

Traversing the ten miles from St. Mark's to the Frey residence, Pastor Werner thought about the Gayle he had known over the decade of his pastorate at St. Mark's. In his mind's eye he could still see her kneeling before him at the altar rail nine years earlier, his hand resting firmly on her head as he said the confirmation prayer: "Gayle, the Father in Heaven, for Jesus' sake, renew and increase in you the gift of the Holy Spirit, to your strengthening in faith, to your growth in grace, to your patience in suffering, and to the blessed hope of everlasting life." And he could still hear her voice responding solidly, "Amen!" He remembered Gayle's laughing, happy face that he had seen so often around St. Mark's during her teen years. After high school, it was off to the U.S. Navy, where she had become a computer technician and a "4/0 sailor"—the highest efficiency rating achievable by persons of her rank. Two years later she married Neil Turner, a Navy flight controller, and the next year Stephen was born. Recently Gayle's parents had proudly informed Pastor Werner that Gayle and Neil were going to have another child and were joining a Lutheran congregation in San Diego.

At the Frey home Pastor Fred (as Werner was affectionately known in the parish) found Gilbert and Katherine Frey numb with shock, scarcely aware of what they were feeling. Gil was downstairs in the den, staring at some program on TV. Fred was amazed at Katherine's charitable attitude. She seemed to be without anger or bitterness, unwilling to blame anyone. "We just don't know what happened yet," she told him. As he left the house, Fred checked his datebook. The church funeral would have to be Sunday afternoon in order to give the Navy Honor Guard and other friends from San Diego opportunity to be present.

Front Page News

The murder story hit the front page Wednesday morning, and further details were published in each subsequent edition. It quickly became topic A in town, and Pastor Werner realized that the funeral on Sunday would be a major item in Monday's paper. He telephoned the newspaper to request that no pictures be taken during the funeral. Otherwise, despite the media hype, Pastor Fred planned to treat this funeral the same as any other at St. Mark's.

Gradually the tragic story unfolded. On her way home from the three-to-midnight shift at the base, Gayle had run out of gas and hitched a ride home. Neil and Gayle then took their other car and filled a gas can at a service station. They took a shortcut on a side road that brought them to within a few hundred feet of Gayle's Honda stalled on the interstate. Neil wanted to go with Gayle to the car, but she insisted that she could take care of herself. She reminded him that she was an expert in martial arts. So Neil drove home as Gayle carried the gas can up the embankment to her car. When she failed to arrive home, Neil returned to the interstate. There he found Gayle's body lying on the front seat of her car, clothes disheveled, a bullet in the back of her head.

Friday's paper broke the news that three men, ages 18 to 22, and one juvenile had been charged with the crime. Only hours after the murder, one of them had been arrested when his attempt to burglarize a house had been foiled by a neighbor. The suspect fired at the neighbor with a .38 calibre handgun, now believed to be the murder weapon. The suspect subsequently implicated the other three in the murder. According to the news article, Neil believed that his pregnant wife had been shot after fighting off attempts to rape her. "It was a brutal act aganst humanity," he was quoted as saying. "They were evil, cruel people. They were out looking for someone to hurt." The coroner, however, reported no evidence of rape.

In another edition a reporter interviewed Gayle's coworkers at the naval base. They spoke of their "sunny, independent friend," who was "at a high point in her life." "Gayle was the leader," said a data-processing seaman. "She was confident, a good organizer, very methodical. She had control of her life."

Pastor Werner was following the developing story and visiting the Freys daily. On one such call he had a chance to talk to Gayle's younger sister, Diane. She told him that something like this never becomes real until it happens to your family. She expressed her feelings of loss and anger. "I do not understand how this happened or how anyone could ever be so cruel," she said. "Gayle was such a happy and loving person, who touched so many. I'm angry that this was allowed to happen, angry that humanity allows this. I want so much for those who violated Gayle's righ: to life to be punished."

The Navy Hymn

Gradually the funeral service was taking shape in Fred's mind. Rites and services are considered very important in the Lutheran tradition, and St. Mark's was no exception. The church staff—Pastor Werner, Associate Pastor Jerry Jensen, and the organist, Dr. Karl Kreider—consulted on every detail of each service to make sure that all components fitted together harmoniously, right down to the last hymn. Fred had an especially close, collegial relationship with Jerry, whose advice he sought and respected.

Most of the funeral service was prescribed by the Lutheran liturgy, but there were hymns and texts to be selected and a sermon to be prepared. Pastor Werner never gave a eulogy, but he customarily printed in the bulletin a brief life history of the deceased, recounting the relationship of the person to the church. Within those limits he tried to follow the wishes of the family wherever possible. A sermon was beginning to form in his mind, focusing on the anguish God shares with us in such moments of grief, yet pointing beyond the present to God's promise to "make all things new." He thought he could easily tie in the scene that kept replaying in his mind: Gayle's confirmation.

Before finalizing the funeral service, however, Fred made one more visit to the Freys to see if they had any special requests. Katherine suggested some materials, most of which Fred felt he could not use appropriately. What the family most wanted, she added, was for the Navy Hymn to be sung in the service. Fred considered that a sound suggestion.

Back in his study at the church Fred pulled down the hymnal and found the Navy Hymn.

> *Eternal Father, strong to save,*
> *Whose arm hath bound the restless wave,*

> *Who bidd'st the mighty ocean deep*
> *Its own appointed limits keep:*
> *O hear us when we cry to thee*
> *For those in peril on the sea.*

Succeeding stanzas went on to proclaim the Christ whose voice hushed the foaming deep and to praise the Spirit that quieted the waters' angry tumult. Then came the last stanza:

> *O Trinity of love and power,*
> *All trav'lers guard in danger's hour;*
> *From rock and tempest, fire and foe,*
> *Protect them wheresoe'er they go;*
> *Thus evermore shall rise to thee*
> *Glad hymns and praise from land and sea.*

Fred drew a deep breath. "All trav'lers guard in danger's hour"? "Protect them wheresoe'er they go"? How do you include a hymn like that in a funeral for someone murdered on the highway?

"Holy Hannah, Jerry," he shouted to his colleague in the next room. "Look what they've given me to put in the service!" Together they looked at the hymn and talked over what needed to happen Sunday afternoon. Fred's first impulse was not to use the hymn at all. That, however, would mean rejecting the specific request of the family. His second thought was just to leave off the last stanza. Yet with the hymnal open in front of the participants, wouldn't that make the evasion obvious? So Fred suggested tentatively that the best approach might be to tackle the issue head on. Jerry concurred. "It's *the* intellectual challenge to the faith," he remarked.

Fred savored the idea, but he wanted to give more consideration to two questions. First, would tackling the problem of evil meet the family's need? He could check that out when he visited the family Saturday evening before putting the sermon on paper. Second, where *was* God Tuesday morning? Did he have an answer to that? If God is omnipotent, omniscient, and omnipresent, and if "in everything God works for good," as Romans 8 claims, then why didn't God protect *this* traveler "in danger's hour"? Did he have any answer to that?

Early Saturday evening Pastor Werner found the Freys at the motel where Neil Turner and his parents were staying. Stephen, Diane, and several members of the Navy Honor Guard were also there, relaxing together over pizza before the difficult day ahead of them. Fred sat down next to Neil and asked how he was feeling about tomorrow. "I don't want to think about it," Neil replied. "That's why the party." Then he added, "I grew up learning not to hate. Tonight I could kill. And I don't like that. I'm scared of that."

After a short stay Pastor Werner excused himself and drove back to his study. Settling into the chair in front of his word processor, he leaned back and closed his eyes to pray about the task before him.

Disbelief, Numbness, and Anger

There are three things about the death of Gayle Frey-Turner that make it acutely distressing. First, she was young, just beginning to experience the rewards of her career and the joys of parenting. Most of her life should have been ahead of her. We feel outraged when someone like this is cut down in the prime of life. It is such a waste! Second, death came without warning. There had been no illness that might prepare others for this early conclusion to Gayle's life. What was anticipated was quite the opposite: the joy of new birth, not the sorrow of sudden death. Third, it was a violent death, the kind that will surely give the survivors nightmares as they mentally picture the event. No death with dignity here! We know that bereavement under these three circumstances is particularly distressing. We should expect that it will take a heavy emotional toll on family and friends, and that grief work will be a long and arduous process.

Let us begin at the beginning, however, with the impact of Gayle's murder on Pastor Fred. He is her former pastor, but we may assume that he is not particularly close to Gayle. Yet he registers shock on hearing the news: "Gayle murdered? . . . That free spirit? . . . How could it be?" His immediate reaction is *disbelief.*

There is, to be sure, nothing out of the ordinary in this reaction. In similar situations we have all had that "it can't be true" feeling. We should not pass over his response without noticing that it reveals one instance of the way most of us react to tragedies that involve us personally. A relative of a passenger on an ill-fated Delta flight out of Dallas was shown on the evening news crying out, over and over, "Oh, no! Oh, no!" An injured survivor of the air show disaster in Ramstein, Germany, described it as "just like a nightmare. . . . I just kept on saying, 'This is not real. It's not happening.'"[1]

Psychologist Ronnie Janoff-Bulman explains this instinctive denial of tragic news. "Whenever someone becomes victimized by a disaster, whatever its nature, their most basic assumptions about themselves and the world are undermined." These basic assumptions, she says, are that the world is benevolent, controllable, and fair, and that we are invulnerable. These convictions constitute "basic trust," learned in childhood and essential to survival. A child handles traumatic loss by creating a fantasy in which everything is magically restored to the way it was. In adulthood the vestige of this is the instinctive denial manifest in this sense of unreality and disbelief. Recovery from the impact of traumatic events, Janoff-Bulman adds, "requires rebuilding those assumptions."[2]

Pastor Fred's incredulity lasts only a moment—the child in him crying out against what the adult recognizes as the sad truth. Quickly he moves toward the duties reality requires and calls on Gayle's parents. We should not expect so quick a recovery by Gilbert and Katherine Frey, who are far more deeply impacted by the loss of their daughter. Yet Pastor Fred is surprised by their charitable attitude, lacking in anger or bitterness. How can this be explained, especially in light of the statement made in the first chapter that the first phase of suffering can be a time of almost overwhelming feelings? Of course, we also insisted that everyone's response is unique, but the serenity reported here is so far from what might be expected that we need to seek another explanation.

The clue can be found in Pastor Fred's own observation that they were "numb with shock, scarcely aware of what they were feeling." Numbing—a damping down of emotions—is the typical way we deal with feelings that threaten to overwhelm us. Numbing lets the feelings out more gradually over an extended period of time so that the sufferer can deal with those powerful emotions at a manageable pace. Numbing is especially evident in Fred, who remains in the den, "staring at some program on TV." Numbing enables persons to maintain control of themselves, to keep from flying apart. It's what leads people to say at funerals, "He's holding up very well."

In a later visit, when Pastor Fred talks with Gayle's sister Diane, he finds her far from serene. Even in the same family, people are different! Diane's secure, benevolent, and fair world has been shattered also: "I do not understand how this happened or how anyone could ever be so cruel." She responds with *anger,* a perfectly normal reaction to the horrendous deed that has destroyed her sister and violated her own life. It is healthy that she is able to get that anger out and face it honestly. She seems somewhat confused about where to direct the anger, however. Clearly she is angry at the murderers, but before she calls for their punishment, she states, "I'm angry that this was allowed to happen." Her use of the passive voice leaves the target unspecified: Who is it that "allowed" this to happen? Then she adds, "Humanity allows this," but who is this generalized "humanity"? My hunch (it can be no more than that, based on our limited data) is that "humanity" is a surrogate for God. It is God who allowed it to happen, and God is the real target of Diane's anger. She can be honest about her deep feeling of anger, but she doesn't quite dare to direct it at God, where she subconsciously thinks it belongs.

If Diane feels anger, Neil feels *rage:* "I could kill!" Here the target is not in doubt. Those he could kill are obviously Gayle's assailants.

His difficulty is handling that deep feeling. The hatred is so overpowering that he cannot suppress it, as he was taught to do. There are surely also other feelings troubling Neil in addition to rage and hatred. When Pastor Fred asks about his feelings, his initial response is: "I don't want to think about it." One would surmise, however, that he is experiencing not only grief, but also *guilt* for not accompanying Gayle back to her car. Whether or not such guilt is reasonable is irrelevant; again and again the thought will recur, "If only I had . . ." He will feel guilty whether to do so is reasonable or not. In any case, Neil is keeping his emotions in check for the moment through the diversion of a pizza party. That should neither surprise nor shock us. Every mourner needs periodic relief from grief work.

The Navy Hymn

The problem most immediately confronting Pastor Werner is how to handle the ticklish question raised by the words of the Navy Hymn. He seems hesitant to use the occasion of a funeral to address the problem of evil; but he feels obligated to honor the family's request to use the hymn, and he doesn't see how he can do that without addressing the issue that the hymn raises. Perhaps his decision is also being influenced by that brief instant when his own world momentarily cracked. I venture to say that every one of the many times a pastor is confronted by shocking evil, he or she must once again go through a personal resolution of that riddle.

The use of the Navy Hymn in a funeral service for one murdered on the highway does raise the problem of evil about as sharply as anything could. The first four stanzas sing praises to the mighty God who brings order out of chaos, sets limits to the oceans, and commands storms to cease. This is the God Almighty declared by the great creeds. This is the Lord of heaven and earth, for whom "all things are possible [Mark 14:36]." This is the One proclaimed on the bumper sticker, "God is in control." The theological term for this is omnipotence, which means "all-powerful." To this attribute the tradition adds omniscience and omnipresence, but these powers are already implied in the concept of omnipotence. Thus *omnipotence means that there is no feat too difficult for God, nothing God does not know, nowhere God cannot be.* More specifically for our case, this means that *God is totally in control: nothing happens unless God wills it.*

Having said that, we must immediately add a small disclaimer. *God cannot do the logically impossible.* Logical impossibility refers to that which is self-contradictory, like square circles, married bachelors, undying mortals. Such self-contradictory phrases are, of course, meaningless nonsense, mere gibberish. It in no way demeans the divine power to say that God cannot do nonsense! "Nothing which implies contradiction falls under the omnipotence of God," says Thomas Aquinas, and virtually all theologians have agreed.[3]

The Navy Hymn celebrates not only God's almightiness, but also God's *love*. Belief in a God who cares is implicit in the petitions of each stanza, for what help would all-powerfulness be to "those in peril on the sea" unless God cared enough to use that power to "protect them wheresoe'er they go"? The centrality of divine love in Christian faith scarcely needs to be emphasized. The best-known biblical verse is John 3:16: "God so loved the world . . .," an idea voiced frequently in the New Testament, culminating in "God is love [1 John 4:8]." God's love is the Christian accent given to Judaism's confession of God's goodness, justice, lovingkindness, and mercy.

Omnipotence and love, the two divine attributes at the heart of Christian faith, are joined together in the petition of the hymn's final stanza:

> O *Trinity of love and power,*
> *All trav'lers guard in danger's hour;*
> *From rock and tempest, fire and foe,*
> *Protect them whereso'er they go.*

Gayle was just such an endangered traveler, and that inevitably provokes the question, "Where was God Tuesday morning?" Why did not the "Trinity of love and power" use that power to guard and protect this traveler?

The Problem of Evil

Gayle's murder presents us with one more instance of the classic problem of evil, as old as religion itself. Intuitively we sense what logic makes clear: evils like Gayle's wanton killing are incompatible with our belief in an omnipotent and good God. Three basic convictions or premises are involved here, and they cannot all be true together:

- *God is omnipotent:* There is nothing that God is not able to do. (God has all the power needed to have prevented Gayle's murder.)
- *God is perfectly good:* God wills only good and seeks to prevent evil. (God did not will Gayle's murder but sought to prevent it.)
- *There is evil in the world:* Things happen that contradict goodness and that goodness would will to prevent. (Gayle's murder was evil.)

The classic statement of the incompatibility of these three premises was made by philosopher David Hume in the eighteenth century. It may be paraphrased as follows:

- Is God willing to prevent evil, but not able? Then God is powerless (that is, not omnipotent).
- Is God able to prevent evil, but not willing? Then God is malevolent (that is, not good).
- Is God both able and willing? Whence then is evil (that is, evil is then inexplainable).[4]

Hume's three questions correlate with the three premises stated above, each one attacking the validity of the corresponding premise. The upshot is that all three premises cannot be true together. Hume is forcing us to the radical solution of surrendering one of the three premises. It seems we must choose one of the following:

- God's power is limited, so that there are in fact some things God cannot do (like preventing Gayle's murder); or
- God's goodness is limited, so that sometimes God lets evils happen (like murder); or
- things that appear evil really aren't (that is, Gayle's slaying, though apparently evil, is actually good).

The Believer's Dilemma

The solutions above are radical solutions. Can any of them be right? The third option—to deny that Gayle's murder is really evil— immediately offends our sensibility, so we are initially inclined to look elsewhere. Yet it is just as difficult for the believer to surrender divine omnipotence or perfect goodness. We cling to these two attributes tenaciously and not just because Christian tradition has always affirmed God's omnipotence and absolute goodness. The conviction runs deeper, for almightiness and perfect goodness seem to be an integral part of the very idea of God, of the "godness" of God. I have heard people say that a God for whom anything is impossible just isn't God. And with equal vociferousness others insist, "I could not worship a God whose goodness is less than perfect." It seems that omnipotence and goodness are the very essence of deity, and that anything less is not worthy of our worship.

The insistence that both of these attributes are essential to the very meaning of deity leads us to a fourth solution, which is even more radical than the previous three, for if the three premises cannot be true together and if the very definition of God requires both omnipotence and absolute goodness, then we are forced to choose between the reality of evil and the reality of God. The believer is confronted with a deep dilemma: either evil is an illusion or the almighty, good God does not exist. The problem of evil has become an argument for atheism! Indeed, evil has always been the Achilles' heel of Christian faith. "The fact of evil," asserts theologian John Hick, "constitutes the most serious objection there is to the Christian belief in a God of love."[5] Stendhal, the nineteenth-century French novelist, once quipped, "The only excuse for God is that he does not exist."

Radical Solutions

Our initial resistance to the radical solutions of surrendering one or another of the three premises—omnipotence, perfect goodness, or the reality of evil—has driven us toward the even more radical answer of atheism. Perhaps, then, we have been too hasty in refusing to reconsider these premises. Let us examine what it would mean to reject each of them in order to see if one of the resulting positions might commend itself to us.

Limited God

Perhaps God did not intend Gayle's death at all. Perhaps another power caused it against God's will. "There are some things God does not control," claims Rabbi Harold Kushner. "Maybe God does not cause our suffering. Maybe it happens for some reason other than the will of God."[6] If, however, some other power caused Gayle's death and God was unable to prevent it, then there are some things God cannot do, and God has neither all power nor total control. Such a God is not omnipotent in the way we have been defining that term.

As the sales figures of Rabbi Kushner's book demonstrate, many people find comfort in his position that God is not responsible for everything that happens. The burden is removed of worshiping a God who is the reason for every horror that happens in the world. Instead of fearing the austere God who sends us suffering from the heights, we are freed to trust in the compassionate Companion who stands beside us in the depths. A price must be paid for this solution, however, for if God could not guard Gayle on the highway, there is no guaranteed protection for us either. The world is then a less secure home than most Christians would like to believe it to be. The Protector-God is dead, and we have become vulnerable.

If some power other than God is the reason for evil in the world, what power might that be? The possible candidates fall into two general categories: (1) *creatures of God* that use God-given powers for ungodly purposes; (2) *beings uncreated by God* that exist eternally along with God in the universe. The first option is not really inconsistent with God's omnipotence, for what God creates, God can also destroy or recreate, as the biblical story of the flood illustrates. C. S. Lewis will not let the omnipotent God off the hook by passing the buck to the creatures: "Even if all suffering were creature-made, we should like to know the reason for the enormous *permission* to torture their fellows which God gives to the worst of creatures."[7] The word *permission* is the sure clue that what Lewis has in mind is the self-limitation of an omnipotent God, who chooses to permit the creatures to exercise power. That is quite different from the notion of a God who from time immemorial has been limited by the existence of one or more other eternal beings. Hence our first option does not really belong under the category of "limited God." We shall return to this fertile notion of divine self-limitation in the next chapter.

The possibility remains that beside God in the universe there are other eternal powers and that these constitute the source of evil. We immediately think of the gods of Greek and Roman mythology, whose mischievous deeds brought suffering to human beings. Even in classical antiquity, however, few took this polytheistic pantheon seriously.

More significant than polytheism is dualism, in which opposing forces of good and evil battle each other endlessly for control of the universe and each soul in it. The classic instance is Zoroastrianism, dating from the seventh century B.C. In this Iranian religion, Ahura Mazda, the god of light, is locked in perpetual struggle with Ahriman, the god of darkness. Human beings, though little more than pawns, are called upon to enlist on the side of good.

Zoroastrianism has disappeared from the world scene, but its viewpoint lingers wherever survival seems to hang in the balance in the life-and-death struggle between good and evil. I once had a dentist who, after stuffing my mouth with cotton, argued that the only religion true to human experience was one that saw the world as a battleground in the perpetual war between the power of good and the power of evil. This perspective on life finds expression in popular culture through Westerns (black hats vs. white) and the Star Wars films (Darth Vader as the dark side of the Force battling the good side). Dualism surfaces in every political campaign, each party depicting itself in lustrous brilliance while coloring its opponents in the ugliest hues imaginable. In international politics rival countries

stereotype each other as "the evil empire" or "the great Satan."
Dualism runs deep in the human psyche.

Another type of dualism presents the two primordial realities as
creator and chaos, both existing together from all eternity. The
creator struggles to order chaos, but chaos constantly threatens to
burst out, bringing evil in its train. The classic version is the
Babylonian creation myth, in which the creator-god Marduk slays the
sea serpent Tiamat, who symbolizes chaos, and shapes the world out
of her carcass. The religious ritual reenacting this myth linked
Marduk with the king, the cosmic order with the political order, thus
giving an early start to civil religion.

The biblical story of creation (Genesis 1) parallels the Babylonian
myth in numerous ways. "Without form and void" was a common
description of chaos, and "the deep [v. 2]" translates *tehom,* which is
the Hebrew equivalent of Tiamat.[8] It would thus appear that the
biblical narrative is an ordering of the chaos. Kushner reads it that
way and concludes that unordered remnants of the chaos, including
the genetic defect that caused his son's death, are one source of evil in
the world. In the biblical narrative, however, no evil remnants are left
at the end of the six days of creation, for God pronounces that "it was
very good [v. 31]." To further safeguard divine omnipotence against
dualistic heresy, the church much later developed the doctrine of
"creation out of nothing."

Although the Babylonian myth is as archaic as the Zoroastrian
one, it too is reflected in our contemporary experience. Old Testament scholar Walter Brueggeman, speaking at Lancaster Theological
Seminary during the tumultuous era of Vietnam and Watergate,
suggested that Protestants today are more troubled by chaos than by
personal guilt, more concerned about establishing law and order than
finding salvation from sin. A decade and a half later chaos seems even
more threatening, as we confront an AIDS epidemic, burgeoning drug
use and drug-related violence, and runaway pollution of the sea and
sky. The picture of chaos breaking loose in the world seems fright-
eningly real. If that picture is accurate, then monotheistic religion has
underestimated the cosmic threat of evil and the limits of God's power
to contain it.

How do these dualisms relate to the death of Gayle Frey-Turner?
Zoroastrianism would see Gayle as one more casualty in the cosmic
war between the forces of good and evil. Babylonian dualism would
interpret the brutal crime as another eruption of the malignant chaos
that God can never totally contain. Both would see Gayle's murder as

contrary to God's will, an evil that a limited God was unable to prevent.

Unjust God

Christian tradition affirms the perfect goodness of a Creator who cares about the smallest creature, even a sparrow (Matthew 10:29). Perhaps that's too good to be true, however. Perhaps the Ruler of this vast universe isn't really concerned about the fall of a sparrow or the murder of a sailor on a remote planet. Maybe God is indifferent to such minutiae. Maybe God even has a mean streak, as some religious folktales suggest. Maybe evil happens because God is unjust.

Even in the Bible we find protests against God's injustice. "Why does the way of the wicked prosper?" demands Jeremiah (12:1). It is a complaint raised often in the psalms, where God is also accused of sleeping on the job, forgetfulness, breaking the covenant, abandoning God's people, hiding, and remaining silent.[9]

Job accuses God of laughing at the calamity of the innocent while blindfolding the judges and turning the world over to the wicked (9:23–24). He complains that he can't find God. If he could, he would drag God into court to prove God's guilt and his own innocence (chs. 9, 23).

These biblical laments became important to Elie Wiesel in the death camp. "How I sympathized with Job!" he mused. On Yom Kippur he refused to fast. "I no longer accepted God's silence. As I swallowed my bowl of soup, I saw in the gesture an act of rebellion and protest." Later he explained his position: "I did not deny God's existence, but I doubted his absolute justice."[10] This stance of contending with God rather than renouncing God's existence has, in the aftermath of the Holocaust, been taken up by numerous theologians, both Jewish and Christian.

More acerbic is Yossarian's complaint in *Catch-22*:

> "And don't tell me God works in mysterious ways. . . . There's nothing so mysterious about it. He's not working at all. He's playing. Or else He's forgotten all about us. . . . Good God, how much reverence can you have for a Supreme Being who finds it necessary to include such phenomena as phlegm and tooth decay in His system of Creation? What in the world was running through that warped, evil, scatalogical mind of His when He robbed old people of the power to control their bowel movements? Why in the world did He ever create pain?"[11]

Closer to home is the experience of many who have felt and sometimes voiced anger at God because of the unfairness of their affliction. In the case before us, Diane Frey-Turner may well be an example of this. Even the pastor's question, "Where was God Tuesday morning?" amounts to an accusation of divine negligence. It is important to recognize the long tradition behind such protests and to avoid suppressing it in the name of piety.[12] A person who can shout against God's injustice will more likely remain close to God than one who clams up in embittered silence.

Why didn't God prevent Gayle's murder Tuesday morning? Did God lack power to do so, or was God negligent? Any attempt to explain Gayle's death theologically—even the more subtle answers that will be presented in the next chapter—end up surrendering either a little of God's omnipotence or a little of God's goodness. We are, it seems, forced to decide which of these two attributes is more important to the very meaning of God for us—unless we can be persuaded that the appearance of evil is really an illusion.

Illusion

The position of evil as an illusion rejects the third premise: the reality of evil. Cast enough light on anything, said Emerson, and you will see that it is good. This implies that if we could only view Gayle's death in the proper perspective, we would see that it really isn't evil at all.

In order to comprehend this denial of evil, we need a clearer understanding of what *evil* means. Once again let us start with several concrete images. M. Scott Peck begins with a definition offered by his eight-year-old son: "Why, Daddy, evil is 'live' spelled backward."[13] Evil is killing. Evil is anything that threatens to destroy life—physically, mentally, spiritually, or socially. John Roth's image is waste. Evil is activity that wastes human life, that "violates the sanctity of individual persons," that "fails to forestall those results." For Roth the Holocaust is the paradigm of evil.[14] Ethicist Philip Hallie draws his picture of evil from the French word *mal*. Evil is "harm, nothing more, nothing less"; it is "destruction of human life." Like Roth, Hallie finds that inaction to prevent harm is itself "an *act of harmdoing*."[15]

S. Paul Schilling offers a more abstract definition based on concrete images such as killing, waste, and harm. He finds (as does Peck) that he can define evil only in contrast to good:

> Normatively, *good* refers to experiences that are really desirable because they enrich and and fulfill life, while *evil* refers to those that thwart such fulfillment and impede the actualization of value.[16]

Note that Schilling defines evil as an "experience," something one *suffers*, whereas, Roth and Hallie describe it as an "activity," something one *does* or *intends to do*. Evil can be either one. The pointless loss of life that Gayle and her family suffered was an evil experience. The malicious act of taking Gayle's life was an evil deed. Sometimes we have an evil experience without any evil intent (illness, natural disaster); sometimes an evil intention without an evil experience (a foiled crime). It may be confusing, but we use *evil* to apply both to sin and to pointless suffering.

Another important distinction essential to understanding evil as illusion is made by Schilling immediately following his definition. He states: "It is not easy to distinguish between *real* and *apparent* goods and evils." Some experiences that at first appear to be evil turn out for the good, and some things that look evil from one person's perspective are good in the eyes of another. In an episode of the television show *China Beach*, the "donut dolly" who is searching for her brother in Vietnam is overjoyed when a corpse turns out to be somebody else. She is shocked to find herself rejoicing at another's misfortune. It all depends on your point of view. It is a matter of perspective.

John Sanford tells a story from the Eighteenth Sura of the Koran that illustrates the problem of perspective.

> Moses and Khidr are traveling together when they come to a village and Khidr unaccountably sinks all the boats. Moses is shocked at what he regards as an evil, but later he learns that robbers would have stolen the boats, and that Khidr, by sinking them, actually thereby saved them for the villagers. Next Khidr falls upon a young man and kills him, which apparent evil act shocks Moses again, but soon he learns that the young man was about to kill his parents and it was better for him to die this way rather than to become his parents' murderer. Finally Khidr makes a wall collapse, much to Moses' dismay; only later it appears that this discloses a treasure for two orphans.[17]

Now consider Gayle's death in that light. From our perspective, a few days after the event, it certainly appears to be evil, but what unforseen benefits, now unimaginable to us, might time bring? Generalizing from that possibility, could it not be that all events seen from the proper perspective are really good, as Emerson claimed? Perhaps it is true that "all things work together for good [Rom. 8:28, KJV]."[18] If evil is only an illusion attributable to our limited and perhaps myopic perspective, then the problem of evil disappears.

Like the other radical solutions, illusion has its price. That price is the refusal to take evil seriously and the trivializing of horrors like

Auschwitz. Evil as illusion amounts to a denial of people's negative experiences and the substitution of a more optimistic, even Pollyannish, interpretation of those experiences. Who would be so bold as to tell Neil or Stephen Frey-Turner that what happened was really for the good? Who would dare lecture Elie Wiesel on the positive values of death camp experiences? Schilling himself cautions his readers: "We dare never forget that events perceived as evil by the one experiencing them must be treated seriously because they are evil for him [or for her]."[19]

Mystery

Having examined four radical positions on understanding evil (atheism, a limited God, an unjust God, and evil as illusion), the reader may wish to plead, "I just don't know." In circumstances much like those faced by Pastor Werner, Father Joseph Donnelly told his congregation: "We all know that there are no answers—none at all."[20] This response is a radical cutting of the Gordian knot, a refusal to accept the options forced on us by the logic of evil.

Surely there are good grounds for adopting this stance. Religion begins and ends in mystery, so why try to unscrew the inscrutable? We are finite beings with limited minds that have difficulty comprehending even simple realities close at hand. Why should we presume to understand the mysteries surrounding the infinite God, especially the mystery of evil? "For my thoughts are not your thoughts, . . . says the Lord [Isa. 55:8]." Why, then, isn't it enough just to acknowledge in faithful humility that we don't know the answers? Shouldn't Pastor Werner follow Father Donnelly's example in his homily Sunday afternoon?

There is much to commend this stance, and, in any case, reverence before mystery will surely be the first and last word any of us has to say. There is, however, an inconsistency in claiming that we know the God in whom we believe while simultaneously pleading that we don't know the answer to the most powerful objection to that belief. Wiesel states the difficulty through the words of a Polish Rabbi in Buna:

> I know. Man is too small, too humble and inconsiderable to seek to understand the mysterious ways of God. But . . . I've got eyes, too, and I can see what they're doing here. Where is the divine Mercy? Where is God? How can I believe, how could anyone believe, in this merciful God?[21]

Three decades later Eugene Borowitz saw it the same way: "There might well be a limit to how much we could understand about [God], but Auschwitz demanded an unreasonable suspension of understanding."[22]

Pastor Werner knows that if he goes before the congregation and professes mystery, more than a few of his hearers will be whispering, "Cop-out!" Is there any other answer that he can offer without embracing one of the radical solutions?

Chapter 3

Freedom Is No Charade

In the last chapter we traced the source of the "why" question about suffering to the incompatibility among three fundamental Christian assumptions: God's omnipotence, God's absolute goodness, and the reality of evil. To escape *atheism,* toward which this incompatibility drives us, we investigated three radical solutions, each resulting from denial of one of the fundamental assumptions. These positions—*a limited God, an unjust God,* and *evil as illusion*—all took us outside the mainstream of historic Christianity. We then considered pleading *mystery* and found that although this stance is basic to religious faith, it cannot address the objections of those for whom the encounter with evil is itself the roadblock to faith in God. These answers comprise five radical solutions to the riddle of evil.

Chapters 3 and 4 will survey six less radical responses to evil, all of which are solidly rooted in the Christian tradition. Instead of rejecting any of the three basic assumptions, these positions eliminate the contradictions among them by redefining one or the other of the key terms, *omnipotence* and *perfect goodness.*

In the last chapter omnipotence was defined as the exclusive possession of all power and the total control over all events. God's power was absolutely unlimited. The four positions examined in this chapter all assume that God's power is self-limited. In this understanding, God's power is more open, permitting the existence of other powers created by God with their own capacities to shape events. In such a context omnipotence means (1) that all power originates from one Creator-God and (2) that God's power is sufficient to bring about the ultimate accomplishment of divine purposes. The other powers that exist are all part of God's creation, instrumental to the achievement of God's plan. Because they possess genuine power of their own, however, they have the potential to become rival powers. Humans,

31

angels, and nature itself have traditionally been regarded as such powers.

Pastor Werner's funeral homily will introduce us to this view of divine omnipotence and the responses to evil grounded in it.

The God Who Can Do Most Everything

Sunday afternoon before a packed congregation, following the singing of the Navy Hymn, Pastor Werner climbed into the pulpit to deliver the homily. He began by repeating four lines of the last stanza of the hymn:

> O Trinity of love and power,
>   All trav'lers guard in danger's hour;
> From rock and tempest, fire and foe,
>   Protect them wheresoe'er they go.

Then he declared, "If God had done this very thing last Tuesday morning, none of us would be in this place this afternoon." After citing the great tradition affirming God's omnipotence, omniscience, and omnipresence, Pastor Werner quoted Paul's ringing assertion of God's goodness: "We know that in everything God works for good with those who love God, who are called according to God's purpose [Rom. 8:28]." Then he heightened the tension between text and event.

"In *everything* God works for good. . . ." Well, maybe so. But . . . when four young men fall upon, violently molest, and finally kill a young pregnant mother early in the morning hours with no personal malice and with a hunger for evil and destruction, I'm rather sure that it is more of a feeble mind than a huge faith that looks for good in such a moment. Perhaps the most healthy sign of our faith on the one hand and the integrity of our God on the other is to raise these "unspeakable" questions:

If God is everywhere—where was God Tuesday morning?

If God knows everything—where was God Tuesday morning?

If God is all-powerful—why did God permit this awful act of evil violation and of murder?

And, if God works together with us for good—where do we go from here?

In these questions there is no suggestion that God *caused* the brutal deed. It was not God who tore at the clothes of a pregnant mother, not God who pulled the trigger. As surely as God's Son wept over Jerusalem, so surely God, too, has wept with us over Gayle.

What we can't understand is how God "the Eternal Father, strong to save" allowed it to happen. But God turns the question back on us: "Why do I allow *you*, over and over again, to be indifferent and to act in defiance of my will? Are you asking me to treat some one way, others another?"

The very integrity that God grants to us to make free choices is bound up in each individual's freedom to choose to obey or disobey, accept or be indifferent to, comply with or be defiant of God's good and loving will for us and others. In God's very own words: "I call heaven and earth to witness against you this day, that I have set before you life and death, blessing and curse; therefore, *choose life,* that you and your descendants may live, *loving* the Lord your God, *obeying* God's voice, *cleaving* to God [Deut. 30:19–20, emphasis added]."

Why does God allow four young men to live in indifference to and act in defiance of God's loving will? It's for the same reason God has stood aside the thousands of times when we, in the self-centered lives of a freedom run amok, have made decisions and carried out acts that cared little for God's loving will and that made us full-fledged members of the "me first" generation. Remember "I Did It My Way"?

We celebrate our freedom to do our own thing—and we expect God to stand aside. So God did for four men on a highway what we have expected God to do for us. "Choose," God says. And we do! . . . When God gives us freedom, it is no charade. It's the real thing—for all its joy in loving and for all its potential to destroy in hating.

Then where is God now? God's right here now in the aftermath, with us—still partners of choice—working with us for good. What happened is evil and despicable. But the story is not over for any of us, not even for Gayle.

Pastor Werner now pressed toward the conclusion that would involve everyone present in the problem of good and evil:

Every single choice is important. We can no longer simply wink at decisions we know stand in indifference to God's will. When we do it, we tell others it's OK. We join in their partnership against God. . . . If we could but once understand that any act of self-centeredness is potentially a violation of another person somewhere on life's highways, God could be doing well among us as God works with us in all circumstances for good.

And for Gayle, God is here, too! Paul says later in that same eighth chapter of Romans: "I am sure that neither death nor life, . . . will be able to separate us from the love of God [v. 38]." So we break bread and share wine in a foretaste of a banquet we believe Gayle already shares. And we commit her body to the ground—ashes to ashes, dust to dust. But we do it in the sure and certain expectation that God will take this dust, precious to God and to us, scoop it up and breathe into Gayle the breath of eternal life.

Ours, finally, is the God who can do most everything. God grants us the gift of freedom. And God promises us life again just at the very moment we seem to have lost it. "We know that in everything God works for the good with those who love (who choose) God!"

The Service of Holy Communion followed, concluding with the recessional hymn. After the committal service at the cemetery, Pastor Fred joined the family and friends for a buffet supper. One sailor told him, "We were asking those very questions on the way up. We loved Gayle, and we were angry and bitter. We never thought the church would answer those questions." An older couple added, "Those are the things we were always afraid to ask." Overall some seemed stunned, others appreciative.

In Monday morning's paper the funeral sermon, accompanied by a graveside photograph, was a feature item on page one.

Freedom

From the outset Pastor Werner makes it clear that he does not question God's power or goodness; nor does he minimize the evil of what has happened. None of the radical solutions will be entertained in his homily. It is equally clear that he does not hold God responsible for Gayle's murder: "It was not God who pulled the trigger."

His answer to the riddle of evil is at once simple and traditional: evil arises because human beings misuse their freedom. Gayle died because four persons chose to commit a brutal crime. According to this view, God created humans "in the image of God," granting them freedom "to obey or disobey, accept or be indifferent to, comply or be defiant of God's good and loving will for us and others." Evil arises, Werner insists, because people choose the latter. The theological term for this is *sin*, which means any distorting or fracturing of relationships with God, others, and the environing world. Ever since Augustine, human misuse of freedom has been the dominant Christian answer to the problem of evil. C. S. Lewis, who stands in this tradition, estimates that human wickedness accounts for four-fifths of the world's suffering (though he doesn't tell us how he tabulated this statistic).[1]

Attributing evil to human choice doesn't let God off the hook, however. God could grant freedom and still override that freedom whenever human beings threaten to misuse it. It wasn't God who pulled the trigger, but why didn't God prevent the trigger from being pulled? The question posed by Pastor Werner is why God allows evil. Why didn't God intervene?

His own answer is that human freedom is a seamless robe. It cannot be conferred and withdrawn piecemeal and still remain freedom. To retract freedom every time evil consequences threaten would quickly turn freedom into a charade. Why would people even try to make good choices if they could count on God to overrule any bad ones they might make? Divine integrity means that God will not override or retract the gift of freedom, even if we abuse or almost destroy it.

Pastor Werner's homily is a good example of what has come to be called the free will defense. According to this position, God has granted us freedom so that we might respond to God and to one another without coercion. Only if people are truly free can their love be genuine; only if they are truly free can God establish a community of love and justice—the reign of God. Even when all the evil attributable to human freedom is taken into account, the argument goes, a world with human freedom and responsibility is better than a world lacking those values.

Within the response of freedom we must draw a distinction between error and sin. Error has long been overlooked as a source of evil, but the frequency with which, for instance, airline disasters are attributed to pilot error has alerted us to the catastrophic potential of error that human freedom makes possible. We err because nobody's perfect. Error is dialing a wrong number, striking the wrong key, misjudging a fly ball, or misinterpreting data. "A Case of Human Error" was *Newsweek*'s headline for the USS *Vincennes*'s attack on Iran Air Flight 655, resulting in the loss of 290 lives.

The exact line between error and sin is not easy to draw, however. When the Soviets shot down an airliner, we called it a crime; when the United States shot one down, we called it an error. *Webster's New World Dictionary* defines error as "something incorrectly done through ignorance or carelessness"; a "mistake."[2] Yet ignorance is no excuse, and negligence is a crime. When President Richard Nixon covered up the Watergate break-in and Lee Iacocca rolled back automobile odometers, each admitted making a "mistake," but were those deeds mere mistakes? It is easier to confess to a mistake than a sin. Self-deception is sin's accomplice.

This brings us to another important distinction, that between sins as misdeeds and sin as a basic inclination. It scarcely seems possible that occasional acts of wrongdoing could account for the mass of evil in the world. The deeper problem is that we are "inclined" toward sin, as a Protestant confession puts it.[3] It's always easier to move in the direction you're leaning!

That toward which we are inclined is not *evil as such* but a *lesser good*, namely, ourselves. We have been leading "self-centered lives" that "cared little for God's loving will," says Pastor Werner. We are "full-fledged members of the 'me first' generation." By using the plural "we," Werner points to a solidarity in sin that parallels our solidarity in freedom. All of us, he is claiming, are inclined to look after number one rather than consider God's purpose or the welfare of others, and that inclination is what brings evil into the world. When we center on self instead of on the true center, we are literally "eccentric," off center, and the world becomes deformed. Paradox-ically, by misusing human freedom, humankind has actually lost some of that freedom: our self-preferring inclination means that we aren't as free to choose impartially as we would like to think. Our choices will always be colored by self-interest. Madison Avenue knows exactly how to exploit this inclination, whether in selling products or candidates. The tradition calls this inclination original sin, and that, Pastor Werner claims, is the basic source of evil in the world, including Gayle's murder.

Can we, however, really ascribe all the evil in the world to humankind? Isn't it misanthropic to heap so much blame on us human beings? (Doubtless some mourners at Gayle's funeral were offended by being told that they shared the blame for her murder!) In order to account for the horrendous evils loose in the world today, isn't something more powerful than human freedom indicated, some superhuman, demonic force? In fact, isn't it surprising that Pastor Werner, in explaining how evil spreads through the world, never once mentioned Satan? A major traditional explanation of evil has been left out of account.

Satan

There are both experiential and biblical reasons for believing in the devil as a cause of evil in the world. Experientially, whenever evil appears to be proliferating in the world, belief in Satan increases. This has been statistically documented for this century's third quarter, at the end of which half the U.S. population professed belief in the devil.[4] Perhaps experience has always been the most effective argu-ment. M. Scott Peck reports that only his personal participation in a satanic exorcism persuaded him of Satan's existence.[5]

In biblical literature Satan is a relative latecomer. The Hebrew common noun śātān, meaning "accuser," is frequently used in the Hebrew Bible to describe God as well as humans, but Satan as a proper noun appears in only three passages, all written after the exile (586 b.c.).[6] In these texts Satan, "the Accuser," is one of God's agents, a member of the heavenly host. The familiar prologue of Job is representative. In the course of making his regular report to God, Satan questions God's boast concerning Job's faithfulness: "Would Job worship you if he got nothing out of it [1:9, TEV]?" Satan proposes to test Job's faith by afflicting him severely, and God agrees to the wager. Here, as in the other two passages, God sets limits on what agent Satan is permitted to do. The strictness of Jewish monotheism left no room for Satan to develop as an autonomous evil power in opposition to God. Satan's work is God's work.

After the exile, two things happened to change this. First, Judaism's basic confidence that "we get what we deserve" (see "Retribution" in chapter 4) was severely strained by repeated foreign conquests. The traditional explanation of the captivity in Babylon was that Jerusalem had "received from the Lord's hand double for all her sins [Isa. 40:2]," but century after century of continuing subservience was too much.

At about the same time Zoroastrianism was spreading throughout the Near East. Zoroastrianism's dualistic cosmic warfare between good and evil offered a way of accounting for Israel's continuing oppression, but this Iranian dualism was incompatible with Jewish monotheism. The myth of fallen Lucifer provided the means by which Judaism, and later Christianity, could embrace a modified dualism. It is a "modified" dualism, because Satan (alias Lucifer, alias Beelzebub, alias the devil) is not a god like Ahriman, the evil god of Zoroastrianism. Satan is an angel, a creature of God, who has misued his freedom to rebel and set up a rival realm. Satan as the source of evil is really a cosmic version of the response of freedom. Like humans, Satan can cause evil only because, and so long as, God permits it.

In the New Testament Satan and his demons everywhere challenge the lordship of God. So strong is their beachhead that Satan is even called "the ruler of this world."[7] Part of the significance of the reign of God heralded by Jesus (Mark 1:15) is the exorcising of the demons and the overthrow of Satan. This was the basis for the teaching of the church during the first millennium concerning the atoning work of Christ. The victorious Christ (*Christus Victor*) has defeated the realm of evil, bound Satan, and set his captives free.

Yet this notion of warfare between God and Satan has always been difficult to reconcile with divine omnipotence. Theologically it is troublesome enough to understand God's gift to human beings of "the enormous permission to torture their fellows" (C. S. Lewis), without adding another whole layer of fallen angels. The Protestant reformers solved the problem by reverting to the notion that Satan can do only what God intends. Thus although Satan may think he's working against God, everything he accomplishes is actually fulfilling God's will. A strange rebellion! A devil that can do nothing but God's will is not only weak but offers no explanation whatever of the reality of evil. If we wish to retain belief in Satan while avoiding dualism, we are once again faced with a strange dilemma: either God gives Satan free reign to cause evil, or else Satan's work is willy-nilly the work of God and hence not really evil at all.

A further reason why religious authorities have been less than enthusiastic about talk of the devil is that Satan provides too easy an excuse: "The devil made me do it." In any case, Christianity has always held each follower responsible for his or her own actions, whether temptation is seen as coming from the lure and enticement of a person's own desire (James 1:14) or from Satan. The devil cannot make anyone do anything without the person's own consent. Pastor Werner's strong emphasis on human responsibility leaves little place for Satan in his homily.

Given the difficulty of reconciling Satan with divine omnipotence on the one hand and human responsibility on the other (not to mention the highly mythological character of Satan-talk), we can see why many people find no help in speaking of the devil. But then, are we willing to blame the human species for all the evil in the world? Or blame God? We can see why faith, seeking to understand genuine evil in the world, waivers between the alternatives of accepting dualism (modified or absolute) or of placing responsibility squarely on the shoulders of humankind. [8]

Natural Order

"Natural order" differs markedly from a Satan explanation in looking for natural rather than supernatural causes for events. Even before the emergence of modern science, human societies built their economies on the reliable structures and repeating cycles that they observed in nature. Crops were planted and harvested, medicinal herbs identified, and sailboats built in accordance with the discovered natural order. Monuments like Stonehenge attest to the importance of these regularities in primitive cultures. Any deviations from these structures and cycles were properly feared because of the devastation they could inflict.

The rise of science and technology has only increased our dependence on the reliability of these patterns in nature. If we could not count on these "laws" of nature, we could not grow, store, and cook our food, erect buildings, heal diseases, or get to work. Dependable structure is necessary for life itself, for the exercise of freedom and responsibility, and for human growth. Hence natural order is an essential dimension of God's gift of life and God's faithfulness to the living.

Yet the same order that is essential to life is potentially dangerous to it and occasionally quite destructive. The wheels of human industry turn on the laws of gravity and inertia; yet gravity brings down planes, and inertia maims bodies. Fire provides energy for human activity but also consumes homes and forests. The water cycle of rainfall, runoff, and evaporation makes our planet habitable but also produces devastating floods. Whatever steps might be taken to render nature more hospitable, some structure is essential; and any structure will have its dangers. "Not even Omnipotence," says C. S. Lewis, "could create a society of free souls without at the same time creating a relatively independent and 'inexorable' Nature."[9]

Once again one might ask: "Why couldn't the Ruler of the universe intervene to hold up falling planes, soften the impact of crashes, quench destructive fires, and lower rivers below flood stage? Why doesn't God pull a miracle whenever the situation requires one?" Yet the frequent interruption of natural order that this would require would soon render it quite unreliable, and the foundational structure on which life depends would soon dissolve into chaos. Whatever life might mean in such a world, it would be radically different from the free and responsible human existence we celebrate in this world. Says C. S. Lewis, "That God can and does, on occasions, modify the behaviour of matter and produce what we call miracles, is part of the Christian faith; but the very conception of a common, and therefore, stable, world, demands that these occasions should be extremely rare."[10]

The upshot is that it is impossible to have a dependable world that does not also involve the risk of destructive accidents. Much of the suffering in this world results from what is called "natural evil," including both natural disasters like earthquakes, hurricanes, floods, and disease, and also those human disasters that happen when human error turns order into injury, death, and destruction.

Character Development

Some of the values we prize most emerge out of the crucible of human suffering. That is a curious fact to which we have so far given little attention. All of us can recall times in our lives that were dreadful while we were going through them, yet are now celebrated as moments of great personal achievement or growth. If this is so, then suffering, far from being all bad, is an essential ingredient in the quality we prize most in human beings, the quality we call character.

Not only do we take pride in such moments in our personal history; we also celebrate the lives of people who have triumphed over misfortune or transformed personal tragedy into profound meaning. The Olympic gold-medal performance of Scott Hamilton takes on added significance because of the childhood disease he had to overcome to skate at all. Helen Keller is respected because of her wisdom forged out of the seemingly impossible obstacles of blindness and deafness. Beethoven's music expresses a depth of tragic meaning arising from his own deafness. The generous nobility of Abraham Lincoln was fabricated out of a life of almost constant adversity. Depth of character, it seems, develops by facing difficult crises and overcoming defeat and pain. By contrast, persons who have encountered few hard challenges often seem shallow.

If this is true, then an important response to the "why" question is that suffering is necessary in order to attain the high value of mature human character. It is a goal that the Creator could not achieve without building into the world the sharp challenges of hardship, defeat, injury, pain, and loss that constitute the stern brew that nourishes character. Mature human personhood, the argument goes, is worth all the suffering required for its accomplishment.

One can find this interpretation of suffering expressed here and there in the Bible. Paul states it in the middle of a famous passage from his letter to the Romans: "We rejoice in our sufferings, knowing that suffering produces endurance, and endurance produces character, and character produces hope [5:3–4]." More often the view is embodied in the story of a great flesh-and-blood personage, like Jacob or Joseph or David, whose youthful rascality is converted through hardship into mature, sensitive wisdom. Perhaps nowhere is this better symbolized than in Jacob's ordeal by the River Jabbok on the eve of his encounter with Esau, the elder brother whom he had tricked out of his inheritance. After wrestling all night with an angel, Jacob receives the blessing of a new name, Israel, symbolizing his transformation. Although Jacob "prevails," he walks away "limping"—the enduring scar of his costly ordeal (Genesis 32:22–31).

The classic expression of this attitude toward suffering was given by poet John Keats in a now-famous letter. Keats objected to the medieval view of this world as "a vale of tears" in which we await a better life to come. As Keats saw it, the world was a different kind of valley. "Call the world if you Please [sic] 'The vale of Soul-making,'" he wrote his brother. "Do you not see how necessary a World of Pains and troubles is to school an intelligence and make it a Soul?"[11]

A full articulation of this response to suffering awaited the twentieth century, with its developmental understanding of human nature unfolding in stages, each presenting new crises that must be addressed by the developing self. By definition, maturity refers to that stage in an organism's life when it reaches the goal of its development. In most creatures, maturity designates a stage of biological fulfillment near the end of life, but in humans maturity also signifies a quality of character that some reach earlier than others and that some never reach at all. Human maturity implies wisdom, responsibility, magnanimity, and sensitivity to the needs of others. These are not traits delivered ready-made at birth, but qualities attainable only through a long process of growth that includes risking vulnerability, surmounting difficulties, and rising above defeat. A person is almost certain to be hurt in such a process. He or she will also be tempted to react to insecurity and defeat by striking out at others, thereby multiplying the evil and suffering in the world.

No one is born mature. "Born mature" is a contradiction in terms, a logical impossibility because it is as nonsensical as "square triangle." If so, then even an omnipotent God cannot create persons who are instantly mature. God could, of course, create a pain-and-risk-free nursery in which to suckle the children of God, but in such an environment human beings would remain perpetual infants. Persons with wisdom to choose and sensitivity to love can only come into being through the long, painful process of maturation that we have described. If the goal of creation is to bring forth selves who can relate to God and one another in this kind of mature way, then this is possible only in a world full of risk and suffering. Yet the prize is worth the high cost necessary to achieve it, in the estimate of those who support this view.[12]

Evil in Service of a Greater Good

The response to evil that we have just examined is a kind of "yes, but" argument. "Yes, there is evil in the world, but look at the higher values that emerge because of it; exclude suffering and evil, and those values would never come into being." In other words, permitting some evil in the world makes possible the attainment of a larger quantity or higher quality of good. "Character building" as an explanation of evil asserts that suffering and sin in the world are the price paid for the higher value of mature human character.

If that claim makes sense, then good and evil are not diametrically opposed to each other in such a way that good will always seek to eliminate all evil; rather, good will see that a little evil can be used as a catalyst to produce a far better world than could be achieved without it. It is an excellent trade-off: some evil for much good. Divine goodness would be less than perfect if God passed over such an opportunity to create a better world. The upshot is that a perfectly good God would not necessarily eliminate all evil but might permit some evil in order to achieve this greater good. In that case the existence of evil in the world is not a conclusive argument against the omnipotent goodness of God.

This is commonly called a "higher good" or "greater good" argument. There are three conditions that must be met if such an argument is to be successful. *First,* the good achieved must exceed the evil incurred in attaining it. It is not enough to observe that some good emerges from an evil situation—it almost always does. The response of "character building" claims that the qualities of character emerging from suffering more than compensate for the suffering and evil necessary for their creation. If it could be shown that mature character is not worth the price in human travail, then the argument would fail. *Second,* the evil in question must be either a necessary means to the attainment of that good or else an inescapable by-product of that good. Suffering, claims the character-building argument, is the necessary means by which character is created. If the suffering under consideration does not contribute to character building, then the argument fails. *Third,* it must be impossible to produce the higher good in any other way. Maturity, it is argued, cannot be had ready-made. If it is conceivable that persons might be born already capable of entering into mature relationships, then the argument fails.

The responses of freedom, natural order, and character building are all examples of the greater good argument, as are the two responses that will be examined in the next chapter. Some persons whose life experiences illustrate the argument may help to make it more concrete. Joni Eareckson, quadraplegic because of a diving accident at age seventeen, wrote an autobiographical account of her journey toward wholeness, which unfolds as a greater-good argument.

> Circumstances have been placed in my life for the purpose of cultivating my character and conforming me to reflect Christlike qualities. And

there is another purpose. Second Corinthians 1:4 explains it in terms of our being able to comfort others facing the same kinds of trials.[13]

In addition Joni sees the accident as vastly increasing her ability to reach others for Christ. "Even one person would make the wheelchair worth all that the past eight years have cost."[14]

Similarly, Catherine Marshall, who was so devastated by the death of her husband Peter Marshall that she doubted God's goodness, later came to see his death as the essential turning point that made it possible for her to multiply his influence through her writing.[15] Both Marshall and Eareckson regard their journeys through suffering as fulfillments of Paul's promise: "We know that in everything God works for good with those who love God [Rom. 8:28]."

By contrast, Rabbi Harold Kushner (see chapter 1), even while acknowledging his personal growth in the wake of his son's death, refuses to regard it as a greater good.

> I am a more sensitive person, a more effective pastor, a more sympathetic counselor because of Aaron's life and death than I would ever have been without it. And I would give up all of those gains in a second if I could have my son back. If I could choose, I would forego all the spiritual growth and depth which has come my way because of our experiences, and be what I was fifteen years ago, an average rabbi, an indifferent counselor, helping some people and unable to help others, and the father of a bright, happy boy. But I cannot choose.[16]

The differences among these three witnesses show us that "greater good" is always a "soft" argument that invites a counter argument. How does one weigh good and evil in order to decide whether the gain is worth the cost? With Eareckson and Marshall the scales balanced one way; with Kushner, the opposite way. What would it take to persuade Kushner that the resulting good offset the instrumental evil? At the time he wrote the paragraph quoted above, his book had not yet been published and he had no idea that it would become a best-seller. Does the fact that millions have read it and tens of thousands have now heard his message in person change his mind about the balance? It has not.

In the next chapter we will conclude our survey of responses to the riddle of evil and see the way one person, namely the author, makes up his mind about the eleven possible responses. First, however, the next chapter will begin with another actual case of human suffering: "God Is Testing Us."

Chapter 4

God Is Testing Us

Chaplain-intern Elsie Muller left the hospital room both inspired and perplexed. She was impressed by the calmness with which Dolores seemed to be facing heart surgery for the second time in four years. Yet Dolores's religious perspective on that situation, in some ways quite traditional, differed markedly from Elsie's. How, the chaplain wondered, could she best minister to one whose beliefs contrasted so sharply with her own?

Chaplain Muller had scarcely finished introducing herself before Dolores Secunda's life story of her thirty-one woeful years began to tumble out. After contracting rheumatic fever in childhood, Dolores suffered her first cardiac arrest at age fifteen. Surgery was prescribed by her physician, but her father refused permission. "Just take it easy and you'll get better," he said; and sure enough, she did feel better for a number of years. Then at age nineteen, just two weeks after her marriage to Tony, she had her second attack. At the birth of each of her three children, she also went into cardiac arrest, but always there were reasons for postponing surgery. At twenty-seven she had yet another attack while waitressing in a restaurant.

This time her heart stopped for three minutes. In spite of what she described as "one-hundred-to-one odds" against success, she agreed to surgery over the opposition of her family, especially of her younger sister Joan. The surgery was complicated, involving the implant of an artificial valve. Post-operative hemorrhaging made it necessary for her to undergo further surgery the same day, and once again she went into cardiac arrest for several minutes. Following a month's recuperation she went home, only to be readmitted twice in quick succession, first with pneumonia, then with kidney failure.

On the very day she was finally discharged, said Dolores, her mother entered the hospital with diabetes. Shortly thereafter her father was fatally struck by a tractor trailer, and Tony's brother was killed in a shooting incident. During the next several years she herself had two malignant tumors removed from a lung, fortunately without any recurrence of malignancy.

Now Dolores was once again facing cardiac surgery, because the implanted valve had been found to be defective. It made her angry that her former surgeon "charged me a fat fee for a faulty valve." She was also "mad at Tony," but she couldn't think of any reason for that.

44

God's Test

Dolores spilled out her story to Chaplain Muller in long but intriguing monologues, scarcely pausing for breath. The chaplain was particularly attentive to Dolores's interpretation of her long history of affliction.

Tony says God's testing us. Sometimes I wonder how much God can test us! My sister Joan says she can't understand it. "You believe in God and don't do anything to hurt anyone intentionally. Why would you have to suffer when there's all these rottener people?" I said, "Hey, I don't know, but I can't do anything about it. Tony says he thinks it's our way of being tested, and I agree with him." Like I told my priest, "I really don't understand it, but I'm going to try to." He said, "That's all you have to do." Maybe I don't have the faith I should. At one time I didn't—that first year after the surgery everything was going crazy and I couldn't figure out why. But now I do have faith, because God has brought us through a lot.

I really think God is testing us, to see how far . . . it's like the kids. They have a way of testing you to see how far you're going to let them get. My little Joey—he wants to be a priest—said, "Mommy, I pray every night. Why is everything going against us?" I said, "Maybe God's testing your faith. You want to be a priest. Maybe God's going to test you."

Dolores's talk of testing reminded Elsie of The Book of Job, which she had studied in her Old Testament seminary course on Wisdom Literature only a few years earlier. Yet God as Divine Stage Manager was a notion Elsie couldn't accept. She viewed God as influencing the world through the power of divine love. She was unwilling to blame God for all the afflictions in Dolores's short life. These thoughts she kept to herself, however, as Dolores continued on without pause.

Joan once said to me, "I don't know why you want to send your kids to Catholic school, because there's no God." I looked at her and said, "You may regret those words, and very soon." A week later Kim, her only child, spilled a pot of coffee over herself and was burned all over her body, everywhere but her face. First thing when she called me she said, "Oh, Dolores, I'm sorry. I hope God'll forgive me." I said, "Oh really? Don't tell me. You'd better tell God." Now she goes to bed every night and prays, "Let Kim live." She says to me, "You said I was going to eat my words. I ate 'em many times. I know there has to be a God now, because everybody says there is." Do you know, Kim doesn't have but one scar the size of a quarter on her foot?

Elsie squirmed in her chair. She knew the Bible spoke of God's wrath, but she was uncomfortable with the idea of a punishing God. The cross, she believed, reveals a God who suffers with us and on our behalf, rather than a God who sends suffering to chastise us. But a hospital room, she thought, was no place for theological debate.

Chaplain Muller did manage to get in some questions about the patient's religious background. Although Dolores's father had belonged to the Church of the Brethren and her mother was Roman Catholic, she herself had been confirmed in the Lutheran church with her best friend. When she married, she became Catholic with Tony, but she admitted to not going to Mass in years.

> I don't go to Mass because one time I fainted, and I'm not going back and faint again. I can't stand the crowds. I feel bad, because I was taught "you have to go to church." But once I get myself together, I'm going to go. If I faint, I faint.

Near-Death Experiences

Chaplain Muller was surprised by Dolores's courage in facing a threatening future. "When they first told me," Dolores admitted, "I was frightened, because I never knew anyone who came out of second heart surgery. But the doctor told me my chances are very good. Leaving the kids alone is what frightens me."

"You aren't afraid of dying for youself?" Elsie asked.

"No," Dolores replied. "I don't know why. I think maybe because I've been close to death, and it's not as bad as people think." She proceeded to describe her experiences during six cardiac arrests, each lasting one to three minutes. All had essentially the same features.

> When I went into it, it was just like I was floating. It was like you're in the country—clouds, blue sky, green grass, flowers. And you just feel like there's no problems at all. I think maybe the reason I'm not afraid to die is because I know it's not going to be ugly and dark and lonely like everybody says. They say when you die you're going to be all by yourself, and it's black and dirty and cold. But after I had the arrest, I never felt that way, because it was beautiful. There was never anything frightening about it. And my husband said I had such a peaceful look on my face. Just like, you know, I don't have to worry anymore. And when I came out of arrest, I felt like I'm a new person, just at ease and relaxed.

Elsie's curiosity was aroused because she had recently read about near-death experiences. When she asked what Dolores knew about that, she replied that she had never heard of anyone with experiences like hers. Elsie's probing produced this exchange:

"While this was going on, did you know you might be dying?"

"Yes."

"Did you feel alone?"

"No."

"Were there people with you?"

"No. All I seen was the sky, but it was just beautiful. Very, very peaceful."

"You didn't see God or Christ?"

"No. I was alone, floating. Anyhow, if I described Christ to you like that picture of him on the wall, you'd say it was just my imagination—we don't know what Christ looks like."

"Did you feel like you didn't want to come back?"

"Once. It was when everything was really going haywire."

"Do you feel that this experience has changed you?"

"I think so, because at one time I was really afraid to die, and whenever I'd tell people I'm not afraid to die, they'd look at me like I'm crazy. And I'm not. I mean, it can't be any worse than it's been."

Dolores seemed to enjoy the chaplain's attention, and her nonstop style made it difficult for Elsie to bring the visit to a conclusion. When finally Chaplain Muller did manage an exit, she left the room intrigued by Dolores's near-death experiences but troubled by her vindictive and manipulative God. Elsie was worried that at a time when any patient would need all the support she could get, Dolores's "testing" God seemed anything but supportive and, in the long run, might actually be quite constricting to her life.

Elsie herself believed the world was a place for free beings to exercise responsible choices, sustained and encouraged by a caring and forgiving God. She knew she didn't have all the answers, but she believed that pain and suffering—even as much as Dolores had known in her short life—were consequences either of bad human choices or nature gone awry. Affliction sent by God to test or punish us simply didn't compute with the God she knew.

Chaplain Muller wondered how she could best minister to Dolores in the days before surgery. Should she try to tell her about the sustaining love of God and attempt to point her toward a less oppressive faith? Or was her role as chaplain in time of crisis to uphold Dolores in her own functioning faith, even though it contradicted Elsie's understanding of the "good news"?

Dolores

What incredible tribulation Dolores has endured in her thirty-one years! Previously we noted how a disaster undermines childhood trust in a benevolent, controllable, and fair world of personal invulnerability.[1] If in her early years Dolores had acquired basic trust, it was quickly subverted by rheumatic fever and the continuing peril of heart failure. Marriage and childbirth, the events in which life is celebrated, became for her moments when death threatened. She was virtually helpless in the grip of forces over which she had little control. The few decisions affecting her life that could be made were mostly exercised for her by others. "I can't do anything about it," she replies to Joan's observation about the unfair happenings in her life. Dolores's world is neither controllable, nor benevolent, nor fair; and she certainly does not feel invulnerable.

If, as Eric Cassell claims, suffering is distress in the face of impending destruction (see chapter 1), then surely Dolores has been schooled in suffering. Cassell warns us not to make such a judgment solely on the basis of external observations, but clear indications of Dolores's inner distress can be found in her rapid-fire retelling of her entire life story and her perplexity about its meaning.

Dolores's search for a reason for her suffering is especially significant in light of Cassell's assertion that finding such a reason can diminish the suffering. It is a way of exercising some control over an otherwise capricious existence.

> Assigning a meaning to the injurious condition often reduces or even resolves the suffering associated with it. Most often, a cause for the condition is sought within past behaviors or beliefs. . . . Physicians are familiar with the question from the sick, "Did I do something that made this happen?" *It is more tolerable for a terrible thing to happen because of something that one has done than it is to be at the mercy of chance.* [2]

In her first long statement, Dolores describes the anguish she felt because of her inability to understand what was happening to her. "That first year after the surgery everything was going crazy, and I couldn't figure out why." Finally she discovered a meaning: "Tony says God's testing us." That interpretation is in striking contrast to her explanation of her sister's suffering. When Joan blurted out, "There is no God"—a conclusion presumably based on the unfairness of Dolores's suffering—Dolores warned her: "You may regret those words, and very soon." Joan promptly received the predicted retribution, which Dolores apparently feels resulted from Joan's lack of faith. The situation conforms to Cassell's observation that some past behavior is usually the reason given for present suffering. (The fact that Kim is the one actually burned is overlooked in Dolores's explanation.)

When it comes to her own troubles, Dolores reaches for a different theological explanation. It is not judgment, because no behavior of hers merits such punishment. Even Joan agrees with that. The only hint that Dolores might consider her own suffering to be divine punishment is her vow to begin attending Mass regularly.

To explain her suffering, Dolores draws on Cassell's other source: strength of belief. Although she attributes "God is testing us" to Tony (deference to authority?), it is doubtful that she would adopt such an explanation were she not already acquainted with it from one or more of her three religious traditions. As Dolores sees it, testing is a trial to examine the genuineness and strength of her faith.

Chaplain Muller is reminded of Job, whose afflictions were visited upon him to test his faith. In the prologue of that book, Satan baits

God: "Would Job worship you if he got nothing out of it [1:9,TEV]?"
Job, insinuates Satan, serves God only in order to receive the good
life. It's a bargain, not true faith, Satan avers. "Take away everything
he has—he will curse you to your face [Job 1:11,TEV]!"

God accepts Satan's wager and places Job in Satan's hands. When
Satan fails to win the bet on the first round, God agrees to a second
round of afflictions. Thus the ordeal tests not only the authenticity of
Job's faith, but also its durability. After the second round Job's wife,
ready to throw in the towel, advises him: "Curse God, and die [2:9]."
But for all his bitter complaining, Job refuses to give up. In the end
God praises his faith, and he is rewarded by receiving double for
everything he had lost. Dolores hopes that she too will find strength
to endure until the test is over: "Maybe I don't have the faith I should.
At one time I didn't. . . . But now I do have faith."

Dolores's God

Dolores has two explanations for human suffering, *retribution* and
testing, one for her sister and one for herself, but both sent by God.
Hers is a very powerful and controlling God. There is enough human
freedom for Joan to renounce God and for Dolores to fail the test of
faith, yet in spite of human actions God always determines the
outcome of events. When Kim spills coffee, burning herself over most
of her body, that is God's doing; and when Kim is healed except for a
small scar, that too is divine providence.

This is an austere God, yet a just one, in Dolores's eyes. Divine
judgment dishes out punishment when behavior merits it but also
shows mercy when repentence earns that. Unlike Job, Dolores does
not rail against the injustice of what God is doing to her. We can
understand why she might be reluctant to complain about God's
justice when we consider how quick she herself was to condemn Joan's
doubts. Yet some misgivings about the justice of what is happening to
her creep into her discourse. Her opening statement, "Sometimes I
wonder how much God can test us!" indicates a feeling that God has
pushed her too far. We recall that later she tried to explain to the
chaplain what testing meant by an analogy that strangely inverted the
parent-child relationship:

> I really think God is testing us, to see how far . . . it's like the kids. They
> have a way of testing you to see how far you're going to let them get.

In this analogy God acts like a mischievous child, pushing us to see
how far we're going to let God go! Is this just a mixed-up analogy, or

is it a Freudian slip, revealing how Dolores really feels about being tested this way?

Her concept of God comes close to that of "Punishing Parent believers" as described by James and Savary:

> Punishing Parent believers . . . see God's rules and commandments . . . as a means of testing people.
>
> God is the authority who created the trial and who will judge each one according to the evidence: the person's thoughts, words, and deeds.
>
> Their preoccupation with punishment, divine retribution, and justice condition Punishing Parent believers to view God as continually looking for reasons to punish people. . . .
>
> They see God, not as a Power Within, but as a judge standing high above them, holding thunderbolts in one hand and the scales of justice in the other. God's face appears cold and severe to them. They might spontaneously want to describe God's face as cruel, but even to think like this would be for them a sin punishable by hell fire. They, therefore, cannot allow it of themselves or others.[3]

There may, however, be another side to Dolores's faith that is just beginning to break out in her near-death experiences. In contrast to life, which she would just as soon leave if it were not for her children, death is not "ugly and dark and lonely like everybody says." (One wonders who this "everybody" is.) Instead, it is "beautiful," "relaxed," and "peaceful," like floating on the clouds amid flowers and green grass under a blue sky. It should be no surprise that God is absent from this idyllic scene, for how could Dolores be at ease and peaceful if her overbearing God were there with her? Yet perhaps God is actually present—not the God who tested her and not the God whose picture hangs on the wall of her hospital room, but a very different God whose presence is expressed in classic symbols of the divine: sky, clouds, and flowers, symbols whose significance Dolores herself may not yet recognize. If Chaplain Muller is looking for resources of grace that can sustain Dolores as she faces surgery, this may be the place where those resources can be found.

Returning from such speculations to the way she in fact talks about God, it is obvious that Dolores's God contrasts sharply with the One in whom Chaplain Muller believes. Dolores's God is immensely powerful and does not hesitate to use that power coercively to reward or punish people or to subject them to trial by ordeal. Although her God is just, Dolores does not speak of God as loving or compassionate. For Elsie, however, those are the words that express the central reality of God and that color everything God does. Elsie is uncomfortable with the manipulation and vindictiveness that Dolores ascribes to God. Such behavior is incompatible with the heart of the God in whom Elsie believes, whose purpose is to empower persons rather than overpower them, who works in the world through the persuasion of love rather than coercion.

As their views of God differ, so do their interpretations of suffering in the world. Although both recognize *mystery* by acknowledging that they don't have all the answers, Dolores's explanations are *retribution* and *testing*, while Elsie's are *freedom* and *natural order*. With such different notions of God and with such opposite interpretations of human suffering, no wonder the chaplain is perplexed about how she can best minister to Dolores! Mystery, free choice, and natural order have been discussed in previous chapters. Now let us examine in further detail the responses of retribution and testing. We will begin with judgment, which is the more deeply rooted and pervasive view.

Retribution

Deeply inscribed in the human soul is the notion that *we get what we deserve*. In Eastern religions this is the law of karma, which dictates that a person's status in this life is the inexorable consequence of that person's behavior in the previous life. The Western counterpart is the doctrine of retribution, which teaches that we get what's coming to us, sooner or later, within this lifetime. It is "the basic biblical view," claims Bible scholar Daniel Simundson.[4] Retribution presupposes a proper balance between human behavior and its reward: good deeds will receive positive rewards and evil deeds will be punished. If retributive justice were perfect, the punishment would fit the crime exactly: "life for life, eye for eye, tooth for tooth," and so on (Exodus 21:23–24). The very word *pain* embodies the concept of retribution, for the Latin root of *pain* is *poena*, meaning punishment. Retribution is part of that childlike assumption previously described by Janoff-Bulman (above, p. 18), according to which life is fair in a trustworthy world. In a fair world, everyone receives his or her just deserts.

Retribution is profoundly embedded in our subconscious minds. We draw on this notion every time we say, "You had it coming to you." Hospital chaplains hear it frequently in the plaintive query, "What did I do to deserve this?" Pastors encounter the same question from perplexed members: "She was always such a good Christian. Why is this happening to her?" More than one cancer patient has told me of a visitor who said, "You must have done something awful to bring this on yourself." I also recall a graduate student and expectant mother who was deeply apprehensive because "my life has been too good." It was as if life's joys had to be balanced by sorrows.

The biblical understanding of retribution is well represented by Psalm 1:

> Blessed are those
>   who walk not in the counsel of the wicked,
> nor stand in the way of sinners . . . ,
> but whose delight is in the law of God,
>   and who meditate on that law day and night. . . .
> In all that they do they prosper.
> The wicked are not so,
>   but are like the chaff which the wind drives away.
> Therefore the wicked will not stand in the judgment,
>   nor sinners in the congregation of the righteous;
> for God knows the way of the righteous,
>   but the way of the wicked will perish.[5]

This conviction that God rewards the just and punishes the wicked is expressed often in the psalms. It even underlies the many psalms of lament that protest God's failure to live up to the law of retribution. Consider, for instance, the complaint to God in Psalm 44:17–19 (NEB):

> All this has befallen us, but we do not forget thee
> and have not betrayed thy covenant;
> we have not gone back on our purpose,
> nor have our feet strayed from thy path.
> Yet thou hast crushed us as the sea-serpent was crushed
> and covered us with the darkness of death.

The psalmist's protest is based on the conviction that God justly rewards the faithfulness of Israel. Later the psalmist calls upon God to "Awake" and carry out the divine justice (v. 23).

Usually we think of retribution as individual, meted out on the particular person who deserves it, as in Psalm 1. In the Bible retribution is more often corporate, however, visited on a whole family or nation. All of us are familiar with the retributive warning appended to the Second Commandment: "I the Lord your God am a jealous God, visiting the iniquity of the fathers upon the children to the third and fourth generation of those who hate me [Ex. 20:5]." When the prophets pronounce God's judgment on the people for breaking the covenant, they warn of a punishment that will fall, not on individual lawbreakers, but upon the entire nation. Retribution is even broader in Eden, where punishment for the sins of Adam and Eve is visited on the entire human race (Genesis 3:16–19). Within the Bible itself, however, there is also protest against penalizing anyone other than the individual wrongdoer. Says Ezekiel, "The righteousness of the righteous shall be upon himself, and the wickedness of the wicked shall be upon himself."[6] Psalm 1 and Ezekiel 18:20 describe a just world; the trouble is that this is not the world we know, nor is it the world depicted by most of the biblical writers.

Although the doctrine of retribution can also be found in the New Testament, it is really undercut by Jesus' message of divine grace. Parables like the prodigal son (Luke 15:11–32) and the laborers in the vineyard (Matthew 20:1–16) teach us that we receive from God far better than we deserve. God, says Jesus, makes the "sun rise on the evil and on the good, and sends rain on the just and on the unjust [Matt. 5:45]." Jesus has a gospel of undeserved grace for a world that is far from benevolent, controllable, or fair. Judgment is postponed until the day of resurrection.

Looking at our own experience, we would have to acknowledge a certain amount of truth in the doctrine of retribution. People who smoke have a far greater than average probability of lung cancer, and people who eat high-fat diets are more likely to develop cardiovascular disease. We also observe that the sins of the parents are visited on the children, for the abused are more likely to become abusers, and children of alcoholics have a unique set of vulnerabilities that others do not have. It goes a giant step beyond those statistically valid generalizations, however, to claim that such consequences are God's punishment. Most people today would see such consequences as the operation of natural laws, more akin to what we have titled natural order than to retribution. Furthermore, to claim that such consequences are divine judgment sets up the danger of blaming the victim, often as a way of excusing ourselves from compassionate feeling and action. We see this most obviously today in the attitudes voiced by some religious groups that starvation in Ethiopia and AIDS in the United States are divine judgment, not to be interfered with by human compassion. Even if there were truth in those claims (and I am not for a minute suggesting that there is), we would still need to heed Jesus' own statement: "I came not to save the righteous, but sinners." Too often Christ's twentieth-century followers proclaim wholeness only for the righteous. When we consider the danger of blaming the victim, which the doctrine of retribution invites, in contrast to the undeserved grace that Christ proclaims, we have to question how much relevance "you get what you deserve" still has in the Christian era.

Testing

Although Dolores was quick to pronounce judgment on her sister, she looked for a different explanation for her own pain and found it in the ancient doctrine of testing. As Elsie rightly recognized, the sufferings of Job were intended to be a test of his faith, to see if he would still trust and serve God even if his goodness were not rewarded. Testing is trial by ordeal, to see if faith is strong and true even under severely adverse conditions. Testing is an unscheduled inspection; it is faith's pop quiz.

More ancient than Job is the story of Abraham's test (Genesis 22). God commands Abraham to sacrifice his firstborn son Isaac. It is a deed requiring Abraham to give up his pride and joy, the child of his old age, his hope for the future. It is an outrageous requirement, which violates the deepest family values and vitiates basic human morality. Is Abraham's faith in God obedient enough to carry out an order that goes against all human sensibility? This is Abraham's trial by ordeal. Like Job, Abraham passes the test; and at the last possible moment God provides an acceptable alternative sacrifice.

Jesus' temptation by the devil in the wilderness is another classic example of faith put to the test (Matthew 4:1–11; Luke 4:1–13). In contrast to the seemingly immoral deed that God required of Abraham, the devil prompts Jesus to do three things that in and of themselves appear to be good: to make stones into bread, to rule over all the nations of the world, and to prove that he is the Son of God. In each case Jesus discerns the difference between human expediency and genuine faith in God, citing the appropriate text from scripture. Having passed the test, Jesus proceeds to begin his ministry. This test of faith is reflected in the prayer that Jesus taught his followers: "And lead us not into temptation [Matt. 6:13; Luke 11:4]," better translated as "Do not bring us to the test [NEB]." What "test" Jesus had in mind is not clear in this context. It may mean temptation to sin or may refer to persecution or some other form of affliction.

Brief references to testing appear throughout the Bible. In Proverbs we read: "Gold and silver are tested by fire, and a person's heart is tested by the Lord [17:3, TEV]." That verse is reflected in 1 Peter: "Even gold, which can be destroyed, is tested by fire; and so your faith, which is much more precious than gold, must also be tested, so that it may endure [1:7, TEV]." Paul takes it for granted that afflictions test the steadfastness of faith in Christ, but he also promises his readers that God "will not allow you to be tested beyond your power to remain firm"; furthermore, God will "give you strength to endure [1 Cor. 10:13, TEV]." The Letter of James, after an opening greeting, launches immediately into a discussion of testing. "Count it all joy, my brethren, when you meet various trials, for you know that the testing of your faith produces steadfastness [1:2–3]." He assures his readers that those who endure their trials will be blessed, for they "will receive the crown of life which God has promised to those who love God [1:12]." Here testing is combined with retribution, for ultimately those who endure the test will receive their just reward.

Testing as an explanation of suffering is still heard today, although less frequently than retribution. In her autobiographical account of her long struggle toward wholeness Joni Eareckson reported several occasions when she felt that her injury was a test of faith. Shortly after the accident she prayed, "Lord, just like Your Word says, I believe my accident came to test my faith and endurance."[7] In a far different setting, Elie Wiesel reported the words of one of his colleagues in Auschwitz: "God is testing us. He wants to find out whether we can dominate our base instincts and kill the Satan within us."[8] Testing as an explanation for suffering is heard less often than it once was, but I suspect that the idea is thought more often than it is voiced by suffering people.

We must remind ourselves that those who accept retribution and testing as explanations for human suffering do not regard these as assaults on the goodness of God, even though they themselves may have wrestled with God's goodness in the process of arriving at such a conclusion. These responses hold that it is just for sinners to be punished and that it is good for faith to be tested. Justice and steadfast faith constitute the greater good served by suffering, and these are ends that could not be achieved without such suffering.

A Configuration of Responses

We have now examined a total of eleven possible responses to the engima of evil. Three of these—a *limited God,* an *unjust God,* and evil as *illusion*—are radical solutions in the sense that they reject one of the three basic assumptions underlying the problem of evil: divine omnipotence, divine goodness, or the reality of evil. *Atheism* takes the even more radical step of rejecting the reality of God, while *mystery* cuts the Gordian knot by claiming that any solution to the riddle is beyond human knowing.

To these five radical positions we then added six moderate positions that adhere to all three basic assumptions while modifying the definition of divine power or divine goodness in such a way that the contradiction between the existence of God and the actuality of evil disappears. Each of these six has a long tradition behind it. Each employs either a free-will argument or a greater-good argument or both. The six are *freedom, Satan, natural order, character building, retribution,* and *testing.*

I believe that this list is exhaustive. If so, any additional position will either be a modified version of one of the eleven or a combination of two or more of them. It should now be possible for the reader to identify a response or cluster of responses that represents his or her position (perhaps with some modifications in wording). Defining such a position should be a worthwhile exercise. By way of illustration, and as a stimulus to the reader's self-reflection, I offer my own configuration of responses. As I see it, this constellation of responses best expresses the central Christian affirmation as it encounters our human experience today.

At the outset I acknowledge some measure of truth in every one of these responses. I will not detail what I find valid in each but will consider *testing* and *retribution* as examples. Although it is impossible for me to believe that the gracious God revealed in Jesus Christ selects persons for affliction as a test or trial, I recognize that the crucible of suffering can temper faith and that crises can lead persons to reexamine the direction of their lives. Regarding retribution, I reject the idea that suffering is divine recompense for wickedness, but I cannot deny the relationship between behavior and consequences. Fatty foods increase the possibility of heart attack, speeders are more likely to have accidents, drinkers run the risk of alcoholism, and so on. These examples are more illustrations of natural order, however, than manifestations of divine retribution.

Moving now to those responses that comprise the core of my configuration, I must begin with *mystery.* Reverence before mystery is our proper posture as we contemplate the finite universe, its infinite source and intricate pattern, and the enigma of iniquity that infiltrates it. And when reason has carried us as far as it can, we shall again have to acknowledge that much remains beyond our grasp. Alan Paton wrote: "There is a wound in the Creation, and it groans and travails until now, and I don't know why."[9] Specifically for myself, I wonder why the creation includes birth defects and cancer and viral infection, and why human freedom was made so vulnerable to malignant ideologies and mob psychology. Some unanswered questions will always remain; the enigma of evil cannot be totally rationalized.

Two further responses are at the core of my own understanding of suffering and evil: *freedom* and *natural order*, which must be seen as interrelated. These two positions, I am convinced, are so much a part of the air we breathe today that they are quite inescapable. All of us conduct our daily lives assuming that we can count on the principle of cause and effect and the regularities of the physical world. Would anyone prefer an undependable world, even if it meant that God would always intervene to make things turn out right? And yet we know that we are sometimes badly hurt by those very regularities on which we have come to rely.

We count on a similar consistency in interpersonal relations. Every day, agreements are made and obligations assumed. We take it for granted that those promises have been made freely and that it is reasonable to hold persons accountable for their commitments. Sometimes we get hurt by that assumption, too. Yet would anyone really prefer a world in which God would always override us whenever we make a bad choice or fail to follow through on our commitments? Do we not prize the responsibility and freedom that go with being human too much to wish for such a world? We really cannot have it both ways. It is impossible—logically impossible—to have an ordered world populated by genuinely free beings in which God would intervene every time something threatened to go wrong. The ordered universe would quickly dissolve into an unpredictable world in which God alone called every shot. My conviction, based on our common human experience as well as scripture, is that we do inhabit a dependable world of responsibility and that God faithfully respects that structure and freedom, even when its evil consequences bring pain to God and injury to God's children.

Closely linked to *freedom*, and presupposing it is *character develop-ment*. I agree with John Hick's judgment regarding a pain-free environment: "A world in which there can be no pain or suffering would also be one in which there can be no moral choices and hence no possibility of moral growth and development."[10] Simone Weil puts it more succinctly: "If there were no affliction we would be able to believe ourselves in Paradise. Horrid possibility."[11] A world in which free persons confront the challenges of hardship, adversity, and loss is essential to the development of those values we most prize as the mark of true humanity. Yet the limited but genuine truth in this response becomes repugnant if it is expected to account for the entire range of human suffering.

Returning to *freedom*, which is the heart of my configuration of responses, I must also acknowledge that the human evil let loose on the planet in this century far exceeds what can be attributed to the sum of individual bad choices. Greed, exploitation, violence, and oppression have run rampant in our time in a way that staggers the imagination, especially when we try to think of ourselves as rational, well-meaning creatures. How do we account for our tendency toward destruction to the point of genocide and even biocide? How do we explain that we are hell-bent on suicide through a nuclear arms race, through pollution of the environment, through stripping away the topsoil on which our food supply depends? We can only answer that God's image in us has become grossly twisted and distorted. Our God-given freedom has turned inward on itself, becoming self-serving instead of God-and-other-serving.

Furthermore, we all too readily give our freedom away to powers larger than ourselves that promise to protect us, deliver us, or give our lives meaning. Erich Fromm, with his eye on the phenomenon of Nazism in the Third Reich, calls this "escape from freedom." The Hebrew prophets termed it "idolatry," noting that we freely create our own idols, then implore them to save us.[12] We surrender our freedom every time we say, "The government knows best," or "I vote with the party," or "America: love it or leave it."

All too often these idolized powers lead us down the road to evil. Until we recognize that evil has this social, systemic structure, we shall never adequately confront it. Power structures, ideologies, and social movements are human fabrications, produced by the creative image of God in us; yet they can utilize their power to captivate and enslave us, thereby undermining the very freedom from which they arose. When that happens, we are no longer the free beings we were meant to be, and the evil unleashed on the earth is multiplied. So we must pray not only "forgive us our sins" but "deliver us from evil." Only as God empowers us and as we open ourselves to that empowerment can we be liberated from bondage to evil and give ourselves to the anticipated reign of justice and peace.

Chapter 5

Christ's Sufferings and Ours

In the last three chapters, we have made very few references to Jesus Christ when looking at the range of possible responses to suffering. Furthermore, the New Testament interpretations of suffering that we cited are largely reiterations of views already enunciated in the Hebrew scriptures. It might seem, then, that Christian faith really has nothing unique to contribute to our understanding of human suffering.

Indeed, were we to search the New Testament for specific answers to why people suffer, not only would we find little that is new, we would discover virtually no interest at all in answering the "why" question. To be sure, some older views are discarded. Retribution, for instance, is specifically rejected in the Sermon on the Mount: "God makes the sun rise on the evil and on the good, and sends rain on the just and on the unjust [Matt. 5:45].[1]" We will look in vain, however, for any brand-new explanation for suffering beyond those already given in earlier scriptures.

We should not conclude from this that the New Testament is not interested in suffering. Far from it! Many passages are exhortations to accept suffering as part of the cost of discipleship: "Blessed are those who are persecuted for righteousness' sake, for theirs is the kingdom of heaven [Matt. 5:10]." Even more important, the New Testament centers on the story of Jesus, at the heart of which is a deeply poignant account of suffering. The Christian message is inextricably linked to the story of Christ's passion, presented as the narrow gate through which come our liberation and healing (which is to say, our salvation). "Suffered under Pontius Pilate" is the one thing the Apostles' Creed has to say about the life of Jesus. Indeed, the account of the last week of Jesus' life, culminating in his crucifixion, is so large

59

a part of the four Gospels that a Gospel has sometimes been defined as "a passion narrative with an extended introduction." (*Passion* comes from the Greek *pathos*, meaning suffering.)

What made this tale all the more startling in its first-century context was the claim of Jesus' followers that their suffering leader was none other than the Christ—that is, the Messiah. "The beginning of the gospel of Jesus the Messiah," we read in the very first verse of the Gospel According to Mark. The reason that claim was shocking was that Judaism included no expectation of a suffering Messiah. The Messiah was to be the agent through whom God would cast out Roman oppression and bring in God's realm, modeled on the golden age of the Davidic kingdom. In the context of first-century Judaism, "suffering Messiah" would have been a contradiction in terms, for a Messiah who suffered the humiliating death of a criminal could scarcely be the agent of a restored Israel. There is abundant evidence in the New Testament that Jesus' followers themselves had trouble understanding why their Messiah had to suffer and die. Only by connecting the Messiah with the "suffering servant" of Isaiah 53 were they able to resolve the seeming contradiction. So far as we know, these early Christians were the first ones in Judaism to make this connection.

The suffering of our Savior is central in the four Gospels, in the letters of Paul, and in the Christian message passed on to us. If the question is "What does Christian faith have to say about human suffering?" then the place for us to begin is with the story of Christ's passion, as we seek to understand how our stories of suffering fit into his story and how his cross illumines the countless crosses of human history.

In this chapter we will focus primarily on the passion narrative as reported in Mark's Gospel, which is widely regarded as the earliest of the four canonical Gospels. We cannot properly interpret the passion apart from its extended introduction, however; so we will begin by identifying some features of the larger gospel account that are essential to understanding the passion.

Galilee

After a brief report of Jesus' baptism by John and of his temptation in the wilderness, Mark introduces Jesus' ministry with this statement:

> Now after John was arrested, Jesus came into Galilee, preaching the gospel of God, and saying, "The time is fulfilled, and the reign of God is at hand; repent, and believe in the gospel." (Mark 1:14–15)

There is a broad consensus among New Testament scholars that verse fifteen is an authentic expression of Jesus' own understanding of his mission. The Synoptic Gospels (Matthew, Mark, and Luke) agree in presenting Jesus as one who perceived himself uniquely chosen by God to announce the imminent in-breaking of God's reign and to call people to faithful response. In Luke's Gospel Jesus states: "I must preach the good news of the reign of God to the other cities also; for I was sent for this purpose [Luke 4:43; cf. Mark 1:38]."

The reign of God would not have been a new idea to Jesus' hearers. In the Judaism of that day, God was the eternal ruler of the world, whose sovereignty could never be overthrown, no matter how much the forces of evil might appear to triumph. In the six long centuries since the Babylonian captivity, however, that reign of God appeared to have gone into eclipse. One foreign power after another had conquered and dominated the once glorious kingdom of David and his successors, regarded as God's vicegerents on earth. The longer this conquest and oppression dragged on, the more Judaism clung to the hope that God's rule would one day again be manifested with power. The time would come, they believed, when the foreign yoke would be broken and a Jewish realm reestablished. In that day God's active rule would become effective, not only in Palestine, but throughout the world. This reign of God, although in one sense a restoration of the Davidic monarchy, would be more than another historical empire, for unlike secular realms that rise and fall, God's reign would have no end. Furthermore, its coming would mean a transformation of history itself: the powers of evil would no longer hold sway, justice and peace would embrace each other, and the Law would be written on the hearts of all. Even nature would be transformed: the calf and the lion would be friends together, and children would play fearlessly over the adder's den (Isaiah 11:6).

This expectation is reflected in the text that Jesus, according to Luke, read when he preached in the synagogue at Nazareth:

> The Spirit of the Lord is upon me,
> because the Lord has anointed me to preach good news to the poor.
> The Lord has sent me to proclaim release to the captives
> and recovering of sight to the blind,
> to set at liberty those who are oppressed,
> to proclaim the acceptable year of the Lord.[2]   (Luke 4:18–19)

Jesus followed the reading with the statement: "Today this scripture has been fulfilled in your hearing [v. 21]." Here preaching good news to the poor, liberating the oppressed, and healing the infirm are linked together as manifestations of the in-breaking reign of God.[3]

Beyond these common beliefs about the anticipated reign of God, ideas varied widely. Some expected it to be inaugurated by a new Messiah; others, by the archangel Michael. Some thought God's reign would be an occasion for sweet revenge against Israel's oppressors. Many believed that there would be a resurrection of the righteous so that they might participate in the new realm of justice and peace; others held that righteous and unrighteous alike would be raised for judgment on that day.

Jesus' listeners heard him proclaim that this long-expected reign of God was now suddenly at hand. It was just around the corner, we might say—so close that you could taste it. The followers could already glimpse the first glow of the dawning new day. It was so near that they were convinced they could see it already breaking forth, not only in the preaching of Jesus, but also in the healings he performed and in his power over demons. "I saw Satan fall like lightning from heaven," Jesus exclaimed as he envisioned the imminent triumph of God over the powers of evil (Luke 10:18). These, he asserted, were "the signs of the times [Matt. 16:3]," the sure indicators that "the time is fulfilled."

If Jesus' hearers were already familiar with the reign of God, they were surely astonished at the way Jesus proclaimed it. He never defined it. Instead, he offered a cascade of parables, many beginning with the phrase, "The reign of God is like unto . . ." Each parable shattered some basic assumption in that popular picture of the expected reign. Jesus said that God is like a housewife who searches diligently for one lost coin and rejoices when she finds it. God is like a father who, when his wayward son returns, throws him a party instead of throwing the rascal out (as family values in that day required). God is like a farmer who pays the farmhands far more than they have earned. This realm of God is not for those who consider themselves righteous, but for tax collectors, harlots, and sinners: "Those who are well have no need of a physician [Mark 2:17]." It is the realm of the poor: "It is easier for a camel to go through the eye of a needle than for a rich man to enter the realm of God [Matt. 19:24]."

The hearer's response to the good news of this upside-down kingdom is to sell everything for the supreme joy of discovering this treasure, this pearl (Matthew 13:44–46). Such a transformation of life is what Jesus meant in calling his listeners to repent in response to the dawning of God's reign. Above all, this means loving God and neighbor as self (Mark 12:29–31). It even means loving our enemies, making peace with our adversaries, forgiving as we have been forgiven.

Another feature of this in-breaking rule of God is the intimate presence of the divine love. This was dramatized in many of the parables and actions of Jesus, but nowhere is it clearer than in the way Jesus himself addressed God. The word he used was *Abba*, an intimate term of affection used in Aramaic-speaking families. Our equivalent would be *Papa* or *Daddy*. Reflecting his own practice of prayer, Jesus taught his followers to pray "Our Father," a prayer combining intimate address to God with petition for the coming of God's reign.

From Galilee to Jerusalem

The good news of the incursion of grace into a sin-sick world, together with the call to transformation in response to its coming, was the cause for which Jesus left home, family, and carpenter shop. "I was sent for this purpose [Luke 4:43; cf. Mark 1:38]." The Gospels report that his message was heard gladly. As he carried his campaign around Galilee and the cities of the Decapolis, his enthusiastic following became so large that he could no longer enter a town but had to preach in the open country and beside the sea. The only negative note was the murmuring of the authorities, who were so threatened by Jesus' message that they began to plot ways to dispose of him (Mark 3:6).

Midway in the gospel story a turning point is reached. Luke records it simply: "He set his face to go to Jerusalem [9:51]." Apparently the herald of God's reign would have to carry that message to the holy city, the city of David, there to confront the powers that be. So the Jesus movement wends its way down the Jordan valley to Jericho and up the hills to Jerusalem, making a triumphal entry on Passion [Palm] Sunday and confronting the authorities in the temple. Quickly the thrill of victory yields to the agony of defeat, as triumph turns into tragedy and the good news of Jesus Christ becomes the story of his passion. Judas conspires to turn Jesus over to the authorities. Jesus and his disciples, for whom the common meal has been so important throughout their journey together, eat one last meal in a secret room. Lifting the cup, he says to them, "Truly, I shall not drink again of the fruit of the vine until that day when I drink it new in the realm of God [Mark 14:25]."

Gethsemane

The poignancy of the passion narrative deepens with each step along the way from the upper room to Gethsemane to Golgotha. In Gethsemane Jesus asks the disciples to wait while he prays.

And he took with him Peter and James and John, and began to be greatly distressed and troubled. And he said to them, "My soul is very sorrowful, even to death; remain here, and watch." And going a little farther, he fell on the ground and prayed that, if it were possible, the hour might pass from him. And he said, "Abba, Father, all things are possible to thee; remove this cup from me; yet not what I will, but what thou wilt." (Mark 14:33–36)

Mark paints a very human portrait of Jesus in Gethsemane. He is "greatly distressed and troubled," as any of us would be in anticipation of the suffering that lay before him. He is "very sorrowful, even to death," as if, in typical human fashion, he were grieving his own imminent loss. This is, indeed, the picture of "a man of sorrows, and acquainted with grief [Is. 53:3]."

He then prays that God might alter his destiny by sparing him the cup of suffering. Along the road from Caesarea Philippi to Jerusalem he had been instructing the disciples concerning his fate and testing their preparedness for the same: "Are you able to drink the cup that I drink, or to be baptized with the baptism with which I am baptized [Mark 10:38]?" Yet now he is asking that he himself might be spared this baptism of fire. It is a very human plea. The Letter to the Hebrews reflects this humanness in describing Jesus as "one who in every respect has been tempted as we are [Heb. 4:15]." Finally, however, Jesus rejects the temptation and yields his will to God: "Not what I will, but what thou wilt."

The Cry of Abandonment

The arrest and trial follow, punctuated by Judas's betrayal, Peter's denial, the disciples' flight, and desertion by the fickle crowd. Jesus is led to Golgotha and crucified; taunting onlookers cry: "Save yourself, come down from the cross!" and "He saved others; he cannot save himself [Mark 15:30–31]." To them he must have seemed a pitiful, powerless pretender.

Mark, the earliest of the Gospels, records only four Aramaic words from the cross: "Eloi, eloi, lama sabachthani?" which means "My God, my God, why hast thou forsaken me?" Once again, we are surprised by the deep humanness of this question, for most of us have asked it in a time of affliction. Here is the same "Why?" that haunts every sufferer; it asks, "God, where are you?" It is Jesus' cry to the One in whom he has placed his faith, an anguished expression of his sense of final abandonment. God's servant is in agony, God's cause appears to be shipwrecked on a cross, and *Abba* is silent.

The reader is perplexed by this final, tormented shout from the cross, which scarcely constitutes uplifting last words from the one we call Savior. The Stoics, contrasting this with Socrates's courageous final speech, scoffed at the pitiful cry from the cross. Luke and John were apparently embarrassed by it also, for they substitute far more heroic last words: "Father, into thy hands I commit my spirit [Luke 23:46]" and "It is finished [John 19:30]."

Some have sought to escape the dilemma by noting that Jesus' words from Mark's Gospel are the first line of Psalm 22, which concludes with faithful words of praise. Yet instead of jumping to its stereotypical ending, we should note that Psalm 22 is a lament, complaining about God's silence in a time of affliction. In any case, as a pastor said after losing his son to leukemia, "You don't sing psalms on crosses!" Instead of papering over the embarassment or fleeing to the resurrection announced in Mark's next chapter, let us linger over these four words to see what meaning they might have for Mark's passion narrative.

We have already noted how human this cry from the cross is! Jesus is one of us, truly our brother in the flesh, for he has been where we have been and experienced the hurts that we have experienced. It's not that he suffered greater pain than any other human being ever did (a dubious claim that Good Friday sermons frequently make), but that he plumbed the depths of human suffering in so many ways that any suffering person can easily identify with him.

There is, to begin with, the physical pain. Crucifixion was a particularly tortuous form of public execution, used by the Romans on foreigners (not citizens) to deter crimes such as sedition, the accusation brought against Jesus. After being scourged and forced to carry his cross (or crossbar) to a public place of execution, the condemned was stripped and affixed to the cross in an immobile position, so that he could not care for his bodily needs, cope with the weather, or even brush away the swarming flies. Death came, usually after many days, as a result of exposure, thirst, or suffocation. Jesus' quick demise was unusual, perhaps due to the severe scourging routinely administered to one convicted of sedition.[4] Those wracked by pain can readily identify with the pain of Jesus portrayed here.

Crucifixion was also a way of publicly shaming the victim. Spectators and those who passed by taunted and jeered the crucified, as Mark's account makes clear. It was doubly shameful for a Jew to die on the cross, "for it is written, 'Cursed be every one who hangs on a tree [Gal. 3:13; cf. Deut. 21:23].'" Because nothing in the traditions of Judaism indicated that the Messiah would meet such a fate, the shame of crucifixion was a particularly difficult obstacle for the early Christians.[5] Any person whose suffering involves shame can identify with the plight of Jesus, exposed to public disgrace and ridicule.

There is, in addition, the experience of abandonment and isolation familiar to so many who suffer. The crowd has turned against him, his companions on the road have fled, those who asked to be always at his side have deserted him in his hour of trial, and even Peter, the one who swore never to deny Jesus, has already done so. Only the women remain, watching from a distance. Most devastating of all, Jesus' most intimate companion, the one he calls Abba, is silent. Those whom affliction has isolated readily identify with this Jesus.

Despair is another part of Jesus' suffering. How, he must have asked, can one hanging on a cross be the instrument of God's reign? The movement to which he had devoted his life seemed to have come to an end. Not only was there no apparent future for the cause that had been his destiny, but it must have seemed that the cause itself was a delusion and his life a waste. It does not take much imagination to see the despair in Jesus' cry of dereliction. Those whose suffering is haunted by despair can identify with that.

Most devastating of all for Jesus must have been the sense of ultimate desolation: abandonment by God. It has been said that a person can endure most anything if he or she knows the sustaining presence of God. In time of distress many of us turn to the reassuring words of Psalm 23: "Yea, though I walk through the valley of the shadow of death, I will fear no evil: for thou art with me; thy rod and thy staff they comfort me [v. 4, KJV]." Yet as every hospital chaplain knows, persons whose wholeness is imperiled by disease or other danger often feel deserted rather than sustained by God. Perhaps this is because of a lingering magical assumption that God will protect the faithful from all ill. Then when disaster strikes, it can only mean that God's back has been turned on us. Whether or not that is the explanation, the disturbing report is that when patients are in the valley of the shadow of death, they feel abandoned by God more often than comforted by God's presence. In this distressing state of alienation from God, sufferers cry out with Jesus: "My God, my God, why have you forsaken me?" They know firsthand what Jesus was going through.

Thus there is a profound identification of suffering persons with Jesus; sufferers who read the passion story with unclouded eyes will find there a reflection of their own plight. Still, what difference does it make that another human being two thousand years ago experienced the same kinds of suffering that we do today? Surely a large multitude of persons from the beginning of history until now would qualify for that dubious honor. It is only because this person holds a unique place in human history and in the hearts of those who claim his name that it matters to us. Paul has stated that uniqueness most succinctly: "God was in Christ [2 Cor. 5:19]." Jesus is, as it were, a window to the very heart of God. "He who has seen me has seen the Father [John 14:9]." In Mark's Gospel, which has given us these dramatically human scenes of Jesus in Gethsemane and on Golgotha, there is never any doubt about this unique relationship to God, for the very first verse tells us that Jesus is "Son of God," and the same words are pronounced by the Roman centurion at the moment of Jesus' death:

> And Jesus uttered a loud cry, and breathed his last. And the curtain of the temple was torn in two, from top to bottom. And when the centurion, who stood facing him, saw that he thus breathed his last, he said, "Truly this man was Son of God."[6] (Mark 15:37–39)

The import of this is that it is not just a person named Jesus who shares our afflictions; but *God* is present in the very depths of our suffering, and our suffering is taken up into the very heart of God. New Testament scholar Wolfgang Schrage writes:

> In all this there is the declaration that Jesus, with his sufferings, is always leading the way for all who suffer, and it is *his* suffering alone that provides a foundation for the certainty that God is to be found here also, and precisely here.[7]

"There was a cross in the heart of God," writes Charles Allen Dinsmore, "before there was one planted on the green hill outside of Jerusalem."[8]

Mark's passion narrative, then, is not just the story of a good man whose suffering resonates to all dimensions of human suffering. That very human cry of abandonment is also God's cry of abandonment, from God to God—from God the Son to *Abba*. It is, to be sure, a deeply paradoxical picture that Mark paints: God taking into the depths of the divine life the very experience of God-forsakenness so typical of human suffering. It is the final step of the incarnation, the endpoint of that trajectory traced by John: "And the Word became flesh and dwelt among us [1:14]." Now God has entered totally into our life.

Theologian Jürgen Moltmann, who asserts that "the only idea of God . . . that can be called Christian is the one that can endure before the face of the dying, forsaken Christ," summarizes the significance of Jesus' cry of abandonment this way:

> On the cross of Christ God cuts himself off from himself. He delivers himself up in order to be ours and to be with us, right into the desolation of God-forsakenness itself. Even in this hell, thou art there. That is the divine truth of Jesus' cry of desolation. And that is why, on the other hand, we cannot shut out any suffering or any loss or any grief from God. . . . Nothing is shut off from God, if God himself has gone through the experience of Christ's cross.[9]

God suffers with us. In Jesus God has so totally immersed the divine being in human life that God can understand with perfect empathy every twinge of our pain, every dimension of our anguish. "Ours is not a high priest unable to sympathize with our weaknesses," concludes the author of Hebrews (4:15, NEB). This is the import of Mark's passion story, culminating in Jesus' cry of dereliction and the centurion's confession. If in the past we have missed the suffering, it is because of an assumption, originating in Greek philosophy and written deep in Christian tradition, that God cannot suffer. The assumption was based on the notion that suffering was a weakness that a perfect being could not have. Yet a god who cannot suffer scarcely accords with the biblical witness and its culmination in the claim that "God is love." It is a strange love that cannot suffer, for the very essence of love is vulnerability to the beloved. Unsuffering love would seem aloof and insensitive. Is not a humble mother who suffers with her children greater than a god who cannot suffer? We are finally beginning to recover the biblical insight, written as deeply into the Old Testament as the New, that God suffers with the people of God. In contrast to classical theology's insistence that God cannot suffer is the suffering God of Christianity. From prison Dietrich Bonhöffer wrote:

> Here is the decisive difference between Christianity and all religions. Man's religiosity makes him look in his distress to the power of God in the

world: God is the *deus ex machina*. The Bible directs man to God's powerlessness and suffering; only the suffering God can help. [10]

How a Suffering God Helps

Yet how does a suffering God help us in our suffering? We would have no difficulty saying how the miracle-working healer of the first half of Mark's Gospel could help, but how does the suffering God of the passion narrative help?

First, God's presence helps us by overcoming the loneliness of suffering. Joni Eareckson, paralyzed from the neck down and immobilized in a Stryker frame, wrote of the comforting presence of Jesus:

> During these difficult midnight hours, I'd visualize Jesus standing beside my Stryker. I imagined Him as a strong, comforting person with a deep, reassuring voice, saying specifically to me, "Lo, I am with you always. . . ." I discovered that the Lord Jesus Christ could indeed empathize with my situation. On the cross for those agonizing, horrible hours, waiting for death, He was immobilized, helpless, paralyzed. . . . Christ knew exactly how I felt! [11]

This power of divine presence is also communicated through two simple songs of faith, deeply ingrained in many of us during our formative years. The first is a hymn: "What a friend we have in Jesus, all our sins and griefs to bear; what a privilege to carry everything to God in prayer." The second is a spiritual: "Nobody knows the trouble I've seen, nobody knows but Jesus." Even when there is no one who can fully share or understand our troubles, Jesus is there.

Eric Cassell claims that a sense of the divine presence contributes to healing: "Transcendence is probably the most powerful way in which one is restored to wholeness." Such wholeness may include physical healing, or it may be the discovery of a new meaning to existence. Either way, this occurs because "the sufferer is not isolated by pain but is brought closer to a transpersonal source of meaning and to the human community that shares those meanings." [12]

If what sufferers feel is abandonment by God, however, it may not help to tell them the story of Jesus' suffering cry of abandonment. In that case we can only follow the trajectory of God's own action and *be* that divine presence with the afflicted. This is what it means to be the body of Christ. "Rejoice with those who rejoice, weep with those who weep," counsels Paul (Romans 12:15). In this way we at least bridge isolation, and we can only hope that in time the sufferer will discern God's care in and through our caring. Our temptation is to feel helpless without, so to speak, the doctor's black bag, to think that our caring makes no real difference. Here we need to listen to the wisdom of Henri Nouwen, who knows the power of "being there" for another:

> The friend who can be silent with us in a moment of despair or confusion, who can stay with us in an hour of grief and bereavement, who can tolerate not-knowing, not-curing, not-healing and face with us the reality of our powerlessness, that is the friend who cares. [13]

The second way that God's presence helps is by giving us strength to endure. Paul informs us that he was afflicted with a "thorn in the flesh." Probably the "thorn" refers to some physical or mental ailment. Some speculate that it was epilepsy, but exactly what it was we do not know. Paul tells us that three times he prayed to God to remove the thorn, but each time he received this answer: "My grace is sufficient for you." The knowledge that God shares our burden gives us added strength to endure.

Two weeks after his eight-year-old daughter, Laura Lue, suffered a painful relapse in her bout with acute leukemia, John Claypool preached a sermon titled, "Strength Not to Faint." It was based on Isaiah 40:31:

> But they who wait for the Lord shall renew their strength,
> they shall mount up with wings like eagles,
> they shall run and not be weary,
> they shall walk and not faint.

Sometimes, Claypool said, God's strength takes the form of ecstasy, enabling a person to "mount up with wings as eagles"; sometimes it is strength for activism, the energy to "run and not be weary"; but sometimes what is needed is simply the strength to "walk and not faint." For Claypool, this was such a time.

> When there is no occasion to soar and no place to run, and all you can do is trudge along step by step, to hear of a Help that will enable you "to walk and not faint" is good news indeed. It not only corresponds to the limits of the situation, it also speaks to the point of greatest difficulty; namely, of being able just to "hang in there," to endure, to be patient, and not to give down one way or the other. . . . This may not sound like much to you, but to me it is the most appropriate and most needful gift of all. My religion has been the difference in the last two weeks; it has given me the gift of patience, the gift of endurance, the strength to walk and not faint. And I am here to give thanks to God for that! [14]

The third way that Christ's empathic participation in our suffering helps is by endowing even the most pointless suffering with meaning. If God goes with me into the valley of the shadow, then my suffering is not meaningless, for we have shared that moment together. Now it is part of God's life as well as mine, and God will treasure it forever in the divine memory. The incarnation means that God is not "above it all" but has entered our lives and incorporated them into the divine life. This is the validity in pantheism's affirmation that "in God we live and move and have our being [Acts 17:28]." If the eternal God is in our suffering, then our suffering is eternally in God, indelibly woven into the tapestry of the divine memory.

The significance of Christ's passion for human suffering then is that God suffers with us; and the good news for suffering people is that God's presence overcomes our isolation by sharing our hurt, that God empowers us beyond our own strength to endure, and that God gives our suffering eternal meaning.

"He Is Going Before You"

It is good news to know that God is with us in the most profound depths of our suffering, but this is not the whole of the good news. If this were the whole gospel, it would amount to surrender in the face of suffering and evil, for then no change in the cause of suffering would result, only empowerment to endure it. The gospel would imply a divine blessing on the world's evils, just as they are. Such a gospel would contradict Jesus' proclamation of the dawning reign of God, in which justice and peace are established, the infirm healed, and the oppressed liberated.

The story of the suffering Christ is not the last word, for the passion narrative ends only provisionally with the cross. The final chapter is the resurrection of Jesus from the dead. The resurrection means first that his cause has been vindicated, his message confirmed. The message of Jesus was that the divine reign was dawning and could even now be touched and tasted. For the earliest Christians, that message was confirmed by the presence of the living Christ, leading them forward and transforming the quality of life in community. Paul spoke of these embryonic communities as "first fruits" or as "downpayment" on the new age that was yet to come.[15] The presence of the Spirit of Christ brought love, joy, peace, patience, kindness, and goodness into the life of the church (Galatians 5:22). Yet even the spirit-filled communities in Christ were a far cry from the promised reign of God, which, at best, was only a fragmentary reality in the world.

We ourselves, like the early church, live between the times of the first in-breaking of the reign of God in Jesus and the complete fulfillment yet to come. In Christian community and in our personal lives we too have touched and tasted the transforming power of Christ, yet we too groan in travail as we await delivery of the new creation aborning (Romans 8:22). God's reign, paradoxically, is both "already delivered" and "not yet arrived." To perceive our situation in the world rightly, we must hold both of those truths in tension.

The joy of the resurrection and the hope for the reign of God do not make us complacent or content with things as they are. Paul says all creation waits "with eager longing" (Romans 8:19). The early church prayed, *"Maranatha!"*—"Come quickly, Lord!"—indicating its yearning that the world in which evil runs rampant might soon be transformed into God's reign of liberating justice.

Resurrection hope leads neither to complacency nor to indifference toward things as they are. The recollection that this world of violence and tribulation is the distortion of God's creation, together with the vision of a new earth in which there will be no tears nor mourning nor pain (Revelation 21:1, 4), prevents us from ever settling comfortably into the world as it is. The expectation of God's reign, symbolized by the resurrection, leads us to critical discontent with the world as it is. Once we have been seized by the dream of a world of justice and wholeness, we can never be satisfied with the world as we now know it. Moltmann well states this implication of Christian hope:

> The resurrection of Christ is not merely consolation in suffering; it is also the sign of God's protest against suffering. This is why whenever faith develops into hope it does not make people serene and placid; it makes them restless. It does not make them patient; it makes them impatient. Instead of being reconciled to existing reality they begin to suffer from it and to resist it.[16]

Once we have caught the vision of the reign of God, we can never be content with things as they are. Robert F. Kennedy's favorite quotation was "I dream things that never were and ask, why not?"

In the wake of the resurrection, then, Christians will cry out against injustice and poverty, against illness and oppression. In the dawning light of God's reign, Christians empowered by the Spirit will struggle to bring into being a little piece of God's realm. In relation to political injustice, economic oppression, and ecological exploitation, the implications are obvious. Christians will always throw their bodies on the side of the victim, not on the side of the oppressor. Empowered by the Spirit, we become the suffering but hope-filled Body of Christ, announcing the dawning of God's reign.

We must not overlook the significance of such a commitment for sickness and health. The reign of God means shalom: wholeness and health. That includes not only interpersonal harmony, but also intrapersonal harmony, and this in turn means wellness. Any theology suggesting that God sends illness for punishment or for any other purpose simply has not taken seriously Jesus' ministry to the sick, with its unconditional commitment to wellness. The Spirit of God works in and through the medical profession for healing. The Spirit of God also works in and through our spirits for healing. This means that God is more than a sustaining presence with us, helping us find peace of mind. If, as Cassell and many others today are claiming, the human person is a psychosomatic unity, then the Spirit of God is divine presence working through our minds for the healing of our bodies as well. We are not talking about a divine intervention in the natural order, disrupting the structures and rhythms of nature. We are speaking instead about utilizing all the resources for healing that the Creator invests in the natural order. We are only beginning to discover what that means.[17] As Shakespeare has Hamlet say, "There are more things in heaven and earth, Horatio, than are dreamed of in our philosophy."

Chapter 6

Resources for Wholeness

In the twenty-fifth chapter of Matthew, Jesus tells a parable of Judgment Day. The King will invite the blessed to inherit the realm prepared for their reward:

> For I was hungry and you gave me food, I was thirsty and you gave me drink, I was a stranger and you welcomed me, I was naked and you clothed me, I was sick and you visited me, I was in prison and you came to me.
> —Matthew 25:35–36

Puzzled by this tribute, the "sheep" ask when it was that they performed such praiseworthy deeds. The King answers: "As you did it to one of the least of these my brethren, you did it to me [v. 40]." By contrast, the "goats," who also question the fate meted out to them, receive the opposite answer: "As you did it not to one of the least of these, you did it not to me [v. 45]."

For those who would follow Jesus, the practical implication is clear. To serve Jesus is to minister to suffering persons wherever we meet them and whatever their affliction. Conversely, to neglect such service affronts and denies Jesus.

Finding opportunity for such ministries is scarcely a problem, for we are surrounded by need in our families, our churches, and our communities. Almost as close, but often hidden, are ghettos of affliction in our cities and in rural America as well. Beyond that are the teeming millions of the poor, the hungry, and the oppressed, populating every corner of our planet. The breadth and depth of human travail are so great that we are tempted, as are the "goats" of Jesus' parable, to sit on our hands, justifying inaction with the question "What can one person do among so many?"

If the extent and depth of human pain is greater than we usually allow ourselves to see, so are the resources of creation and grace that

74

facilitate health and wholeness. In accordance with the mandate of Matthew 25, it is our responsibility as followers of Jesus to enlist these resources for the healing of hurting humanity and of the earth. Cassell describes three broad categories of resources for ameliorating suffering: (1) personal resilience and the ability to redirect life, (2) help that comes from other people, and (3) "meaning and transcendence."[1] Following his outline, in this chapter we will identify personal, communal, and religious resources for coping with suffering. In the process we will discover that these resources are ultimately inseparable from each other.

Personal Resources

Human beings have an amazing power to spring back from adversity and illness, a capacity we customarily refer to as resilience. Physicians have long been familiar with this and have given it the technical name *vis medicatrix naturae*, "the healing power of nature." René Dubos describes this self-healing power:

> The mechanisms of *vis medicatrix naturae* are so effective that most diseases are self-terminating. . . . Recovery depends upon the mobilization of the patient's own mechanisms of resistance to disease."[2]

Those words appear in the introduction to Norman Cousins's book describing how he recovered from a usually fatal degenerative disease, ankylosing spondylitis, by actively participating in his own treatment, including especially the use of humor. Cousins concludes: "I have learned never to underestimate the capacity of the human mind and body to regenerate, even when the prospects seem most wretched."[3]

The human capacity to regenerate includes more than the ability to rebound from diseases. Unlike the so-called lower animals, we cannot grow new limbs or other body parts, but we do have wondrous ingenuity in compensating for such losses. In 1980 mountain climber Tom Whittaker lost his right foot in an automobile accident that nearly took his life. Only his importunity persuaded the surgeons to reconstruct rather than amputate his other foot. After a lengthy convalescence, Whittaker began counseling other patients in their adjustment to handicaps and eventually organized the Cooperative Wilderness Handicapped Outdoor Group. Once, while giving kayak instruction to a spine-injured man, he saw tears rolling down the man's cheeks. Whittaker began to apologize for pushing him too hard, but the man interrupted: "You don't need to apologize. This is the

first time I've felt alive in two and a half years." Today, nine years after
his accident, Whittaker is preparing to climb Mount Everest, using a
high tech artificial right foot. If successful, he will be the first
handicapped climber to perform this feat.[4] Whittaker is but one
illustration of the way in which the human spirit triumphs over
handicaps.

More often, however, an injury or loss makes it necessary for a
person to redirect his or her creative energies into new channels.
When an auto accident compelled Doris Day to give up her youthful
dream of a dancing career, she redirected her artistic talents into
singing and acting. Cassell notes that such redirection can take place
whenever there is "loss of relationships, loves, roles, physical strength,
dreams, and power."

> It is . . . as though an inner force were withdrawn from one manifestation
> of a person and redirected to another. If a child dies and the parent makes
> a successful recovery, the person is said to have "rebuilt" his or her life.
> The term suggests that the parts of the person are structured in a new
> manner, allowing expression in different dimensions. If a previously active
> person is confined to a wheelchair, intellectual pursuits may occupy more
> time.[5]

Designed into our very nature as human beings, this ability to rebuild
our lives is part of what it means to be created in the image of God.
Human beings, of course, do not create "out of nothing"; but using
the shattered fragments of their own lives as raw material, suffering
persons fashion new lives from the shards of the old.

This creative ability to bounce back or to adapt by redirecting life
is especially characteristic of "survivors," claims Bernie Siegel, basing
that finding on his experience with "exceptional cancer patients."[6]
Other traits that appear to enhance survival include confidence, self-
esteem, and self-reliance. Those who, like Cousins, insist on main-
taining control over their own treatment do better than those who
become docile patients. In order to maintain control, it is important
for survivors to identify goals for their lives. "He who has a 'why' to
live can bear almost any 'how,'" says Siegel, quoting Nietzsche. Siegel
is convinced that persons with such a "survival" profile have a greater
chance of coming through a life-threatening illness, and that even
where that does not happen, the quality of their lives will be
enhanced.

These characteristics of the survivor personality can be learned,
Siegel has discovered. Change is difficult, he acknowledges, because
remaining a victim is easier than the painful process of change.

Nevertheless, Siegel has found two ways in which such change can take place. The first he calls "carefrontation": sharing honestly with another person or with a support group that combines caring with confrontation. The second way is a regular discipline of meditation, including "visualiz[ing] yourself as you want to become." Visualization is effective because it penetrates to the unconscious level, where significant change takes place. Even writing, such as journaling, can be a type of meditation.

In summary, each of us has vital personal resources for coping with illness, injury, or any other form of affliction; and these powers can be enhanced through a support group, or the caring confrontation of a friend, or the personal practice of meditation. Any congregation that is concerned about holistic health can construct its educational and pastoral life in a way that will enhance survivor traits, encourage meditation, and nurture support groups.

Communal Resources

"Recovery from suffering," states Cassell, "often involves help, as though people who have lost parts of themselves can be sustained by the personhood of others until their own recovers."[7] That is a truly biblical insight, for we are exhorted to "bear one another's burdens [Gal. 6:2]," and we are reminded that being bound together in the body of Christ means that "if one member suffers, all suffer together [1 Cor. 12:26]" and that we "weep with those who weep" as well as "rejoice with those who rejoice [Rom. 12:15]." Within the Christian community's resources for ministering to suffering people, we will examine personal, face-to-face ministries, then support groups, and finally outreach groups.

Face-to-Face Ministries

There are numerous ways in which individual persons can be healing resources for one another. The simplest is the ministry of listening. Anyone who has suffered personal trauma needs opportunities to vent feeling and to objectify the event by telling the story many times over. Research on grief has demonstrated the value of one person sharing his or her sorrow with another: Siegel reports that "those who bore their grief alone had a much higher-than-average rate of illness, while those who could talk over their troubles with someone else had no increase in health problems."[8] It is critically important, claims Dr. Bessel zan der Kollk of the Massachusetts

Mental Health Trauma Clinic, that survivors of disasters share their grief and avoid isolation.[9] Often "not knowing what to say" keeps persons from calling on the bereaved or seriously ill. Not what we say, however, but how empathically we listen is the measure of effective ministry.

Equally simple is the ministry of touch. Siegel states that "skin starvation"—"a literal separation from life, when touching stops"—is frequently experienced by elderly persons, the severely ill, and those recovering from surgery.[10] I suspect that skin starvation is even more widespread than Siegel acknowledges. Isolation often accompanies suffering of any kind; hence, touching, holding hands, and hugging become doubly important. This should come easy for adherents of a religion that places high value on the body, which is "a temple of the Holy Spirit" according to Paul (1 Corinthians 6:19). Because the body is God's good creation, because "the Word became flesh," and because we are bound together in the body of Christ, we should have no trouble practicing a ministry of touch. Yet, oddly, many Christians are squeamish about touching.

Indeed, we must acknowledge that obstacles to human contact go beyond speech and touch. Although it is almost instinctively human to reach out to those in need, something in us holds back from contact with the seriously ill and those affected by personal tragedy— even if they are close friends. Why is this? Partly, we don't like being reminded of our own vulnerability, but also any relationship is altered when tragedy strikes either party. The friendship cannot continue at any depth until that event is acknowledged. Such an acknowledgment requires risk and effort; hence, even old friends tend to avoid encounters and put off calling "until the right occasion comes along." If the affliction is bereavement or divorce, then an additional obstacle arises: how to relate to a single person where once there was a couple. Often it is the suffering person who breaks the ice by issuing an invitation or giving permission to talk about what has happened. Sometimes, however, it is the sufferer who puts up a wall.

> Most persons facing a life-threatening disease would like to think of themselves as having the courage to face alone what lies ahead. Somehow it seems almost cowardly to let others in on our troubles. Hell should be endured privately. We'd rather be caught dead than parade our self-pity before others. [Unfortunately,] the consequence of this "quiet endurance" often serves to increase the anxiety level for all.[11]

Yet such game-playing does go on, frequently within families. If a moment of candor breaks through, the result is almost invariably an intimacy that establishes a new depth of relationship for all involved. The sufferer with a more healthy attitude will reach out to others for support, recognizing that suffering need not be borne alone and that others seek ways to help.

The ministries we have been talking about are lay ministries. A congregation's resources will be severely limited if this ministry is left only for clergy to perform. The clergyperson's task is to see to it that an effective network of ministry is operating and that volunteers receive training to support this ministry. It is also necessary that the expectations of the congregation about clergy roles be altered accordingly.

Support Groups
We have already mentioned the value of support groups. Existing organizations in which some level of intimacy has been established, such as an adult class or choir, can be support networks for their members; but more helpful is the group that is intentionally formed as a support group, and most effective of all is the group organized around a particular need. Alcoholics Anonymous is the classic example of the latter, but there are also groups for parents who have lost a child (Compassionate Friends), for women who have had a mastectomy, and for children of alcoholic parents, to name but a few. After a 1987 airplane crash in Detroit, survivors organized Flight 255—The Spirit Lives On. Sixteen months later a team from The Spirit Lives On returned to Detroit's Metropolitan Airport to console the families of those lost on Flight 103 over Lockerbie, Scotland. The operative principle in these organizations is that help is best given by those who have been through the experience themselves, provided that the caregiver not project his or her affliction on the recipient and not use the occasion as a means to his or her own healing.

Congregations can host such established groups as Alcoholics Anonymous or Compassionate Friends, or they may organize groups around needs they perceive within the church or community. In response to a request from a widower that something be done for persons who had lost a spouse, a group called Doorways was organized in St. Mark's United Methodist Church, Mount Joy, Pennsylvania. It began with fifteen persons from several churches and the community who met once a month and used the study booklet *Doorways: Living Through the Death of a Spouse.* [12] Leadership emerged from the group itself, and activities were planned. Soon the group burgeoned to one hundred active members, some coming from great distances.

Some years before that a similar organization for divorcing persons was started in nearby Lancaster. Highland Singles, sponsored jointly by a congregation and a social agency, also began with about fifteen members who were in various stages of separation and divorce. Feeling that they were misunderstood and had been treated like lepers within the church, the group members organized for mutual support and to educate the larger church about the problems and needs of divorcing persons. One of their first projects was a workshop to educate area clergy on the topic of "divorce as a suffering event." The organization has evolved into a social and support group for about seventy-five single persons, most of whom are separated, divorced, or widowed.

Outreach Groups

The mandate of Matthew 25 would not be fulfilled if Christians ministered only to the sick and hungry within their own congregations. Ministry to suffering people must reach out to the hungry, the imprisoned, the strangers beyond the church's walls, especially to the pockets of pain that exist within the United States and beyond our borders. One thinks immediately of the homeless on our streets, the poor in the countryside, and refugees wherever they find asylum. Yet these are only the most obvious clusters of persons in need. Fortunately, the church has a long tradition of reaching out to such persons.

Church people were among the first to recognize the growing problem of homelessness in America. Organizations too numerous to tell have arisen for the purpose of providing food, clothing, and shelter for the homeless, often utilizing church facilities. Just as support groups within churches have reached out to serve needs in the larger community, so outreach groups have often proved to be good therapy for those participating. Howard Friend, Pastor of Gladwyne Presbyterian Church, which provided initial support for Trevor's Campaign (a movement in Philadelphia to help the homeless begun by eleven year-old Trevor Ferrell) observes:

> People are discovering the healing power in involvement. This community, like other [affluent suburbs], has a lot of depression. People's primary self-treatment is to pleasure themselves—go on vacation, buy a dress, redo the living room. I believe that depression is really resistance to pain. Something is needed to break it open. Exposure to the pain of the homeless life is wrenching, but it breaks the depressive cycle. There's something about *connection* with the people. [13]

While some groups work to meet immediate need, others seek to address the problem of homelessness itself. The organization Harbadult in Lancaster, Pennsylvania, purchased an old hotel and renovated it to provide single-occupancy dwellings. In hundreds of communities in the United States and overseas, Habitat for Humanity is renovating old houses and building new ones for low-income housing. Church people provide the backbone for most such groups, and many churches have committees or task forces working on such projects. Unfortunately, all these efforts combined have not succeeded in reversing the tide of homelessness, especially among children, and that can lead people to give up in cynicism. Frank Ferrell (Trevor's father) has an answer for that: "If I had a lifeboat at the sinking of the Titanic, I would have filled the boat, not asked, 'What good does it do when there are so many?' "[14]

The churches have also played a major role in resettling refugees in this country. From the DP's of World War II to the Vietnamese and Cambodian refugees of recent decades, churches have taken responsibility for housing and feeding the displaced and for helping them make the transition to meaningful participation in an alien culture. In the 1980s numerous congregations, at considerable risk, turned their churches into sanctuaries for Guatemalans and Salvadorans seeking asylum from war, genocide, and the death squads of Central America. These congregations were seeking to obey the Word of God above all human regulations:

> Do not mistreat foreigners [ger in Hebrew] who are living in your land. Treat them as you would a fellow Israelite, and love them as you love yourselves. Remember that you were once foreigners in the land of Egypt. I am the Lord your God. (Leviticus 19:33–34, TEV)

Davie Napier, commenting on this passage, observes that "there is no suggestion of concern about how and why the ger [alien, foreigner] is among us."[15] Other congregations have helped refugees travel on the "overground railroad" from the Rio Grande to the St. Lawrence, where they find asylum in a land that is more hospitable to Central American refugees than is the United States.

These congregations have rendered valuable assistance to the suffering oppressed of the Third World. Yet the flow of refugees across the Rio Grande, like the tide of the homeless in our cities, continues to increase (as of January 1989). There is a clear message in this for the churches: If, despite our best efforts to assist the victims, the problem continues to grow, then we must address it at its source. Any response short of that lacks genuine compassion. Where people are dying because of a dangerous intersection, it is ridiculous to set up a first-aid station on the corner; what is called for is a march on city hall to insist on a traffic light. Similarly, if the number of refugees and homeless is increasing despite our best efforts to assuage their condition, then what is needed is not more shelters and sanctuaries, but a prophetic insistence that our society address the root causes of the problems.

Thus, compassion inevitably leads to advocacy, and the church's mission to the poor and marginated of society inescapably involves us in political action. U.S. Protestants are much better at charity for the dispossessed than addressing the causes of their dispossession. We dare not compliment ourselves on our compassion when our actions may only make it easier for a society to live with the evils it has spawned.

Religious Resources

We have been exploring intra-personal and inter-personal resources for healing. We now turn to transpersonal resources—the healing power that comes from God. In opening up this dimension we are, of course, focusing more directly on the source of wholeness implicit in the personal and communal resources already identified.

Cassell, who calls this dimension *transcendence,* claims that it is probably the most potent medicine of all for healing human suffering. Transcendence has this efficacy because it places suffering "within a coherent set of meanings" and locates the sufferer "in a far larger landscape." In other words, the context of meaning that religion provides confers significance and value on both the suffering event and the one who suffers it. In this final section we will first look at the way in which seemingly meaningless events of suffering can be redeemed in value; then we will examine ways in which the resources of God's grace can become means for coping with the distress of human suffering.

Redeeming the Event

"The meaning of a word," said linguistic philosopher Ludwig Wittgenstein, "is its use in a sentence." That is, the context in which a word is embedded gives the key to its meaning. This is why a dictionary definition often seems vague until a concrete illustration shows how the word is used. For instance, "Coke bottle" gets its meaning from its use in the production, distribution, and consumption of soft drinks. In the film *The Gods Must Be Crazy,* when a Coke bottle falls from an airplane, the aborigines are puzzled. Their culture offers no context for understanding what it is. The surprising uses to which they put the bottle, which have nothing to do with Coca-Cola, provide much of the humor for the viewer (who, of course, knows what a Coke bottle "really" is). Soon the members of the tribe begin fighting over it, even using it as a weapon, until finally the tribal council decides to get rid of "the evil thing." As this amusing tale shows, the context provides the clue not only to what something is but also to its value or worth.

Much of the anguish of suffering arises because the sufferer's context of meaning—religious or otherwise—has no adequate place to put the affliction. Like the Coke bottle dropped into the Bushman culture, the affliction doesn't fit into the sufferer's world, that is, into the set of meanings that give that person's life its significance and worth. The suffering event then either shatters the person's world or undermines the meaning of the sufferer's life within that world.

The long road back to wholeness involves finding a way to redeem the event, to give it significance within the overall religious framework of meaning that undergirds life. Because of the incongruity between the suffering event and the framework of meaning, this rebuilding process requires a change either in the way the suffering event is perceived or in the surrounding framework that interprets it. For a person of faith, the adjustment in religious orientation may be minor, but sometimes it requires a complete reconstruction of a person's shattered set of beliefs.

When the suffering event can be incorporated into the sufferer's religious faith without undermining it, the movement toward wholeness is enhanced. "Suffering is reduced when it can be located within a coherent set of meanings," says Cassell. "Assigning a meaning to the injurious condition often reduces or even resolves the suffering associated with it."[16] In the extreme circumstance, the potentially threatening event is regarded merely as a challenge. In that case, by Cassell's definition, there is no actual suffering. Much depends on the endangered person's orientation toward life. That is why Cassell insists that a diagnosis of suffering can be made only by the person directly involved, not by an outside observer.

More often, however, struggle and pain are involved in wresting meaning from tragedy; and a person is usually well along in his or her suffering work before finding any positive significance in the suffering.

One way or another, converting pain into meaning is an important step in coming to terms with the affliction and moving beyond it. "When you suffer a misfortune," says Siegel, "you are faced with the choice of what to do with it. You can wring good from it, or more pain."[17] Erect a monument, advises zan der Kollk, or write a book. "Transform grief into action."[18] The Vietnam Memorial has become such a monument for many, and Rabbi Kushner is but one of thousands who have written a book for the purpose of transformation. Karen Quinlan's family built a hospice and named it for Karen. Others have converted the energy of pain into a campaign to eliminate its cause. Bonnie Light organized Mothers Against Drunk Driving. Sarah Brady, whose husband was wounded in the assassination attempt on President Reagan, leads the campaign for handgun control. It seems important that sufferers play an active role in redeeming the event, for meaning is as much created as discovered.

Erecting some kind of monument can be a very therapeutic step in the process of arriving at acceptance and moving beyond a consuming preoccupation with the past. This is, in effect, a "greater good" in action. The original suffering is not usually interpreted as sent from God to bring about this greater good (although sometimes it is) but rather "with the help of God we can salvage some good out of the pain that has occurred." It may be dangerous to cite some well-known instances as those in the previous paragraph, for most of us will, at best, succeed in erecting a few little memorials that seem wholly incommensurate to the pain and loss. We should also beware of making this an "ought," to be laid on ourselves or anyone else. Blessed is the one who can bring meaning out of his or her pain!

The Resources of Grace

Even at a time when no positive good can be found in the suffering a person is enduring, however, faith in God can be a profound source of strength. Through the centuries of Christian existence, the community of faith has found ways by which believers are brought in touch with the One who is their creative and re-creative source. These include the sacraments and rites of the church, prayer and devotional disciplines, forms of worship, and the Bible itself.

All of us know stories of persons who, in time of stress, have found great comfort in one or another of these resources of God's grace. It is said that Martin Luther, in the frequent moments when he was tempted to despair, reminded himself, "I am baptized." Many have been strengthened in time of danger by recalling the lines from the Twenty-third Psalm, "Even though I walk through the valley of the shadow of death, I fear no evil; for thou art with me; thy rod and thy staff, they comfort me [v.4]." This is but one of hundreds of biblical verses from which different persons have drawn sustenance. Others have been helped to get through difficult times by a simple prayer of Reinhold Niebuhr: "Give me the courage to change what can be changed, the serenity to accept what cannot be changed, and the wisdom to know the difference." I recall a seminary professor, blind and bedridden in the last days of his life, who found consolation in singing with a friend the scores of hymns that he had memorized in the course of his life. What these illustrations make clear is that it is easier to draw on spiritual resources that are already well worn than to discover God's grace for the first time in a moment of desperation—although that also does happen!

Nowhere is the sustaining power of these resources of grace more evident today than among Christians in the Third World, from which those of us in the First World have much to learn. We will therefore conclude our survey of personal, communal, and religious resources by seeing how faith empowers the poor and oppressed in their suffering. In such situations Christians discover that their struggle is placed in the larger drama of the redemption that is narrated in the Bible and celebrated in the church's worship. The events in the divine-human story that are especially meaningful include the exodus, the Babylonian captivity, Jesus' flight to Egypt as an infant, his proclamation of release to the captives and liberty to the oppressed, and his identification with the poor, the outcast, and the imprisoned.

Mary's Magnificat, recited frequently in the liturgies of many churches, is an especially powerful text, with its reversal of natural human hierarchies:

My soul magnifies the Lord,
and my spirit rejoices in God my Savior,
for God has regarded the low estate of his handmaiden. . . .
God has shown strength with his arm,
God has scattered the proud in the imagination of their hearts,
God has put down the mighty from their thrones,
and exalted those of low degree;
God has filled the hungry with good things,
and the rich God has sent empty away. (Luke 1:46–53)

Marie Assaad, an Egyptian Coptic Christian, comments on the significance of this text:

Mary offers the greatest song ever sung . . . the song that is filled with the assurance that with God nothing is impossible. God can use us to reverse the state of affairs in our world of disorder, hunger and death, injustice, militarism, nuclear destruction. God can make us agents of shalom. God can commission us to prepare for a world where the lion will lie with the lamb and the rich will be accountable to the poor.

In this text God's option is not only for the poor, but also for women who are often the poorest of the poor.[19]

Charles Villa-Vicencio, head of the Department of Religious Studies at the University of Cape Town, tells how traditional liturgical symbols are juxtaposed with symbols of oppression in South African worship:

> The cross of Christ as a symbol of first-century Roman repression is, for example, sometimes flanked by rubber bullets and empty teargas canisters, symbols of repression in the townships of South Africa.

Villa-Vicencio goes on to describe the significance of the Lord's Prayer in this context:

> To pray for one's daily bread is to affirm the right to eat and the dignity of work; to forgive sins is to recognize the importance of communal relations; to request deliverance from evil is to express resistance to evil structures and destructive people. To pray for God's kingdom to be made manifest on earth is to acknowledge an inherent relationship between prayer and social action.[20]

No wonder that visitors to Third World churches find these congregations to be far more alive spiritually than their counterparts in the United States! Commenting on the comfort of U.S. churches, an African bishop remarked, "You don't *need* God in your country." By contrast, churches under daily persecution turn to their faith for power to "keep on keepin' on." Our sisters and brothers in the Third World have much to teach us about the supporting strength of faith in time of suffering.

The most powerful sustenance of all is the sense of God's immediate presence in the midst of suffering. Teresa Sosa, victim of Argentinian tyranny, has left this witness:

> They began to torture me early in the morning. Naked and with my skin wetted down, I was tied to the *parilla*. . . . They tortured me with electrical shocks on the most sensitive parts of my body.
>
> After a while I lost consciousness. When I came to, I was lying on the floor, on a small mattress, and I was bleeding profusely. I was three months pregnant at the time.
>
> A doctor treated me; I was given injections to stop the bleeding. Then they came for me again, to torture me. . . .
>
> Jesus is with me in prison. *He* is tortured with me. *He* is my last hope![21]

Teresa Sosa was deliberately isolated as part of her torture treatment. Yet she was not alone. Jesus, himself tortured before his crucifixion, is tortured with her. And, in a very real sense, the whole community of the faithful is with her also. Teresa Sosa's witness gives new depth of meaning to Cassell's affirmation: "The sufferer is not isolated by pain but is brought closer to a transpersonal source of meaning and to the human community that shares those meanings."[22]

This chapter has been written from the perspective of readers who are seeking to be instruments of God's wholeness. It is important for those of us who would be healers to acknowledge that we too are vulnerable, however. At one time or another each of us will be the person suffering. It is vital in such times that we be able to draw upon these same resources for restoring our own wholeness.

The personal, communal, and religious resources we have been considering are, of course, not independent of each other. The capacity to rebound from adversity and rebuild our lives is part of our divinely created humanity. Instead of calling this remarkable ability "the healing power of nature," physician Richard C. Cabot prefers to name it *vis medicatrix Dei*, the healing power of God.[23] Similarly, the healing touch of one person with another is always more than "merely human" caring; it is the healing touch of the Great Physician. Some persons will be able to give or receive on one level, others on another; and we should allow for such individual differences, discerning the various gifts that each member of the Body of Christ has to bring. There are, of course, further resources beyond those mentioned here: the support of family, the regenerating power of music, revitalization through exercise, to name but a few. Whether or not they are recognized as such, all can be channels for the healing grace of God.

Notes

Chapter 1—Hurting and Wholeness

1. *Webster's New World Dictionary of the American Language*, 2d college ed., s.v. "pain." Emphasis added.
2. *Random House Dictionary of the English Language*, 2d ed., s.v. "suffering."
3. Eric J. Cassell, M.D., "The Nature of Suffering and the Goals of Medicine," *The New England Journal of Medicine* 306 (March 1982): 639–45.
4. Ibid., 642.
5. Ibid., 640. The key sentences in Cassell on which this definition is based are these: "Suffering occurs when an impending destruction of the person is perceived; it continues until the threat of disintegration has passed or until the integrity of the person can be restored in some other manner. . . . Most generally, suffering can be defined as the state of severe distress associated with events that threaten the intactness of the person."
6. Elisabeth Kübler-Ross, *On Death and Dying* (New York: Macmillan, 1969).
7. *Webster's New World Dictionary*, s.v. "suffering," "to experience pain, harm, injury, loss, etc."; cf. S. Paul Schilling, *God and Human Anguish* (Nashville: Abingdon, 1977), 10, "to undergo physical or mental pain, distress, injury, or loss."
8. Cassell, "Nature of Suffering," 641.
9. Ibid., 643.
10. Elie Wiesel, *Night,* trans. Stella Rodway (New York: Discus Books, published by Avon, 1960), 44.
11. Harold S. Kushner, *When Bad Things Happen to Good People* (New York: Schocken Books, 1981).
12. James LeMoyne, "Testifying to Torture," *New York Times Magazine* (5 June 1988): 44–66.
13. Priscilla Padolina, "Our Presence Among the Poor," *New Eyes for Reading: Biblical and Theological Reflections by Women from the Third World,* ed. John S. Pobee and Bärbel von Wartenberg-Potter (Geneva: World Council of Churches, 1986; Oak Park, Ill.: Meyer-Stone Books, 1987), 37–40.
14. *Cassell's New Compact Latin Dictionary,* s.v. "oppression."
15. Cassell, "Nature of Suffering," 644.

Chapter 2—Where Was God Tuesday Morning?

1. "Air Show Survivors Say Crash Was like Nightmare," *Intelligencer-Journal*, Lancaster, Pa., 9 March 1988.

2. Reported in Daniel Goleman, "Emotional Impact of Disaster: Sense of Benign World Is Lost," *New York Times* 26 November 1985.

3. Thomas Aquinas, *Summa Theologica*, Ia, Q. 25, art. 4.

4. See David Hume, *Dialogues Concerning Natural Religion* (New York: Social Sciences Publishers, 1948), 198.

5. John Hick, *Evil and the God of Love* (New York: Harper and Row, 1966), ix.

6. Harold S. Kushner, *When Bad Things Happen to Good People* (New York: Schocken Books, 1981), 45, 29.

7. C.S. Lewis, *The Problem of Pain* (New York: Macmilian, 1940; Macmillan Paperbacks, 1962), 89, modified in accordance with Lewis's proposal in his footnote on the same page; emphasis added.

8. *The Interpreter's Bible*, 12 vols. (New York: Abingdon-Cokesbury, 1952), 1:467.

9. Psalms 35:23 and 44:23; 42:9; 89:39; 44:9–19; 89:46 and 143:7; 35:22 and 109:1.

10. Elie Wiesel, *Night*, trans. Stella Rodway (New York: Discus Books, published by Avon, 1960), 43, 55–56, 80.

11. Joseph Heller, *Catch-22* (New York: Simon and Schuster, 1955), 178.

12. See Pierre Wolff's readable little volume, *May I Hate God?* (New York: Paulist Press, 1966).

13. M. Scott Peck, *People of the Lie: The Hope for Healing Human Evil* (New York: Simon and Schuster, 1983), 42.

14. John K. Roth, "A Theodicy of Protest," *Encountering Evil: Life Options in Theodicy*, ed. Stephen T. Davis (Atlanta: John Knox Press, 1981), 8–9.

15. Philip Hallie, *Lest Innocent Blood Be Shed: The Story of the Village of Le Chambon and How Goodness Happened There* (New York: Harper and Row, 1979; Harper Colophon Books, 1980), 22, 85, 110, 124.

16. S. Paul Schilling, *God and Human Anguish* (Nashville: Abingdon Press, 1977), 10.

17. John A. Sanford, *Evil: The Shadow Side of Reality* (New York: Crossroad, 1986), 8.

18. This is one of those passages where translation makes a significant difference. The KJV states that "*all things work* together for good" (emphasis added), which reads like a denial that anything is really evil, but the RSV, NEB, and TEV agree that it is God who works for good *in* all things, which implies that God is always seeking to bring good out of evil.

19. Schilling, *God and Human Anguish*, 10.

20. *Intelligencer-Journal* (Lancaster, Pennsylvania), 8 September 1978. Further into his homily, Father Donnelly did give an explanation not unlike Pastor Werner's, which shows how difficult it is to live with not knowing.

21. Wiesel, *Night*, 87.

22. Eugene Borowitz, *The Mask Jews Wear* (New York: Simon and Schuster, 1973), 99.

Chapter 3—Freedom Is No Charade

1. C.S. Lewis, *The Problem of Pain* (New York: Macmillan, 1940; Macmillan Paperbacks, 1962), 89.

2. *Webster's New World Dictionary*, 2d college ed., s.v. "error."

3. See *The Heidelberg Catechism*, eds. Allen O. Miller and M. Eugene Osterhaven (New York: The Pilgrim Press, 1963), Q. 8.

4. Clyde Z. Nunn, "The Rising Credibility of the Devil in America," *Listening: Journal of Religion and Culture* 9 (1974): 84–100.

5. M. Scott Peck, *People of the Lie: The Hope for Healing Human Evil* (New York: Simon and Schuster, 1983), 184.

6. 1 Chronicles 21:1; Job 1–2; Zechariah 3:1–2.

7. John 12:31; 14:30; 16:11; cf. 2 Corinthians 4:4.

8. I have opted for the latter position and tried to explain how this can be so in Richard F. Vieth, *Holy Power, Human Pain* (Bloomington, Ind.: Meyer-Stone, 1988), 59–85.

9. C.S. Lewis, *The Problem of Pain*, 29.

10. Ibid., 33–34.

11. *The Letters of John Keats*, 4th ed., ed. M.B. Forman (London: Oxford University Press, 1952), 334–35.

12. The theologian most often associated with this response to suffering is John Hick, who first elaborated his position in *Evil and the God of Love* (New York: Harper and Row, 1966). An excellent summary of his position is Hick's brief essay, "An Irenaean Theodicy," published together with critiques and a response by the author in *Encountering Evil: Live Options in Theodicy*, ed. Stephen T. Davis (Atlanta: John Knox Press, 1981), 39–68.

13. Joni Eareckson with Joe Musser, *Joni* (Grand Rapids: Zondervan, 1976), 226.

14. Ibid., 228.

15. Catherine Marshall, *A Man Called Peter: The Story of Peter Marshall* (New York: McGraw-Hill, 1951), 259–60.

16. Harold S. Kushner, *When Bad Things Happen to Good People* (New York: Schocken Books, 1981), 133–34.

Chapter 4—God Is Testing Us

1. See above in chapter two, "Disbelief, Numbness, and Anger," page 18.

2. Eric J. Cassell, M.D., "The Nature of Suffering and the Goals of Medicine," *The New England Journal of Medicine* 306 (March 1982): 644; emphasis added.

3. Muriel James and Louis M. Savary, *The Power at the Bottom of the Well:*

Transactional Analysis and Religious Experience (New York: Harper and Row, 1974; a Collins Associates Book, 1974), 122.

4. Daniel J. Simundson, *Faith Under Fire: Biblical Interpretations of Suffering* (Minneapolis: Augsburg Publishing House, 1980), 21.

5. From *An Inclusive-language Lectionary: Readings for Year B.* Copyright © 1987 Division of Education and Ministry, National Council of the Churches of Christ in the U.S.A.

6. Ezekiel 18:20; cf. Jeremiah 31:29–30; and Deuteronomy 24:16. For a more detailed exposition of the biblical doctrine of retribution, see Simundson, *Faith Under Fire*, 17–41.

7. Joni Eareckson with Joe Musser, *Joni* (Grand Rapids: Zondervan, 1976), 59.

8. Elie Wiesel, *Night*, trans. Stella Rodway (New York: Discus Books, published by Avon, 1960), 56.

9. Alan Paton, *Knocking on the Door: Shorter Writings*, ed. Colin Gardner (New York: Charles Scribner's Sons, 1975), 286.

10. John Hick, "An Irenaean Theodicy," *Encountering Evil: Live Options in Theodicy*, ed. Stephen T. Davis (Atlanta: John Knox Press, 1981), 47.

11. *The Notebooks of Simone Weil* (London: Routledge and Kegan Paul, 1956), 294.

12. See especially Isaiah 44:9–20.

Chapter 5—Christ's Sufferings and Ours

1. Cf. Luke 13:1–5 and John 9:1–3, but contrast Mark 2:5, which seems to imply that the paralytic was afflicted because of his sins.

2. The quotation is from Isaiah 61:1–2, except for "to set at liberty those who are oppressed," which is from Isaiah 58:6. "The acceptable year of the Lord" is probably a reference to the Jubilee Year, a year to "proclaim liberty throughout the land to all its inhabitants," including the cancelling of debts and the release of those enslaved (Leviticus 25).

3. A similar set of signs is offered by Jesus to the disciples of John when they ask, "Are you he who is to come, or shall we look for another?" (Matthew 11:2–6).

4. *The Interpreter's Dictionary of the Bible*, s.v. "crucifixion."

5. Ibid.

6. In the Greek original, there is no article before "son of God."

7. Erhard S. Gerstenberger and Wolfgang Schrage, *Suffering*, trans. John E. Steely (Nashville: Abingdon Press, 1980), 168.

8. Charles Allen Dinsmore, *Atonement in Literature and Life* (Boston and New York: Houghton, Mifflin and Company, 1906; Cambridge, Mass.: The Riverside Press, 1906), 232.

9. Jürgen Moltmann, *Experiences of God*, trans. Margaret Kohl (Philadelphia: Fortress Press, 1980; London: SCM Press, 1980), 16.

10. Dietrich Bonhöffer, *Letters and Papers from Prison*, enlarged edition, ed.

Eberhard Bethge (New York: Macmillan, 1972; London: SCM Press, 1953, 1967, 1971), 361.

11. Joni Eareckson, with Joe Musser, *Joni* (Grand Rapids: Zondervan, 1976), 107.

12. Eric J. Cassell, M.D., "The Nature of Suffering and the Goals of Medicine," *The New England Journal of Medicine* 306 (March 1982): 644.

13. Henri J. M. Nouwen, *Out of Solitude: Three Meditations on the Christian Life* (Notre Dame, Ind.: Ave Maria Press, 1974), 34.

14. John Claypool, *Tracks of a Fellow Struggler: How to Handle Grief* (Waco, Tex.: Word Books, 1974), 55, 62.

15. 2 Corinthians 1:22; 5:5 ("earnest" in the KJV, "guarantee" in the RSV).

16. Moltmann, *Experiences of God*, 12.

17. See, for instance, "Body and Soul," *Newsweek* 62 (November 1988), 88–97, and Bernie S. Siegel, M.D., *Love, Medicine & Miracles* (New York: Harper and Row, 1986); both of these develop further some fundamental implications of Cassell's thesis that body and mind is a false dichotomy. Harold Kushner, by implying that God can heal the mind but not the body, falls into the same Cartesian dualism that Cassell finds so misleading for the medical profession.

Chapter 6—Resources for Wholeness

1. Eric J. Cassell, M.D., "The Nature of Suffering and the Goals of Medicine," *The New England Journal of Medicine* 306 (March 1982): 644.

2. Norman Cousins, *Anatomy of an Illness as Perceived by the Patient: Reflections on Healing and Regeneration* (New York: W.W. Norton and Co., 1979), 16.

3. Ibid., 48.

4. *Intelligencer-Journal*, Lancaster, Pa., 11 January 1989, sec. A, p. 4.

5. Cassell, "Nature of Suffering," 644.

6. Bernie S. Siegel, M.D., *Love, Medicine, and Miracles: Lessons Learned about Self-healing from a Surgeon's Experience with Exceptional Patients* (New York: Harper and Row, 1986), 161–204.

7. Cassell, "Nature of Suffering," 644.

8. Siegel, *Love, Medicine, and Miracles*, 187.

9. "The Cruelest Kind of Grief," *Newsweek*, January 2, 1989, 22.

10. Siegel, *Love, Medicine, and Miracles*, 189.

11. Donald C. Wilson, *Terminal Candor* (Lititz, Pa.: Sutter House, 1978), 15.

12. Marna B. Williams, *Doorways: Living Through the Death of a Spouse* (Nashville: Graded Press, 1987).

13. Private interview, April 4, 1984.

14. Private interview, April 4, 1984.

15. See B. Davie Napier, "Hebraic Concepts of Sanctuary and Law," *Sanctuary: A Resource Guide for Understanding and Participating in the*

Central American Refugees' Struggle, ed. Gary MacEoin (San Francisco: Harper and Row, 1985), 33–38.

16. Cassell, "Nature of Suffering," 644.

17. Siegel, *Love, Medicine, and Miracles,* 198.

18. "The Cruelest Kind of Grief," 22–23.

19. Marie Assaad, "Reversing the Natural Order," *New Eyes for Reading: Biblical and Theological Reflections by Women from the Third World,* ed. John S. Pobee and Bärbel von Wartenberg-Potter (Geneva: World Council of Churches, 1986; Oak Park, Ill.: Meyer-Stone Books, 1986), 27.

20. Charles Villa-Vicencio, "South Africa: A Church Within the Church," *Christianity and Crisis* 48 (January 1989): 463–64.

21. *Witnesses of Hope: The Persecution of Christians in Latin America,* ed. Martin Lange and Reinhold Iblacker (Maryknoll, N.Y.: Orbis Books, 1981), 100–1. *Parilla* means "perch"—a wooden beam suspended horizontally between supports at each end, like the perch in a bird cage.

22. Cassell, "Nature of Suffering," 644.

23. Richard C. Cabot, M.D. and Russell L. Dicks, B.D., *The Art of Ministering to the Sick* (New York: Macmillan, 1936), 130.

Bibliography

Cassell, Eric J., M.D. "The Nature of Suffering and the Goals of Medicine." *The New England Journal of Medicine* 306 (March 1989): 639–45.

Chaffee, Paul, et al. *Spirit Awakening: A Book of Practices.* Edited by Paul Chaffee and Judith Favor. San Francisco: Northern California Conference of the United Church of Christ, 1988.

Frankl, Viktor E. *Man's Search for Meaning: An Introduction to Logotherapy.* Boston: Beacon Press, 1959, 1963. Classic work on meaning and hope in relation to suffering.

Hall, Douglas John. *God and Human Suffering: An Exercise in the Theology of the Cross.* Minneapolis: Augsburg, 1986. Excellent introduction to the topic.

Kushner, Harold S. *When Bad Things Happen to Good People.* New York: Schocken Books, 1981.

Lewis, C.S. *A Grief Observed.* New York: Bantam Books, 1961, 1976. Lewis's journal recording his own struggle in the wake of the loss of his beloved wife.

————. *The Problem of Pain.* New York: Macmillan, 1940. Lewis's early treatise on the problems of suffering and evil.

Simundson, Daniel J. *Faith Under Fire: Biblical Interpretations of Suffering.* Minneapolis: Augsburg, 1980. Brief and readable volume on the variety of biblical interpretations.

Vieth, Richard F. *Holy Power, Human Pain.* Bloomington, Ind.: Meyer-Stone, 1988. A fuller development of the author's views on suffering and evil.

Weatherhead, Leslie D. *The Will of God.* Nashville: Abingdon Press, 1944, 1972. An essay many find helpful in understanding suffering in relation to God's will.

Wiesel, Elie. *Night.* Translated by Stella Rodway. New York: Discus, 1960. First-hand account of survival in a Nazi death camp.

Wolff, Pierre. *May I Hate God?* New York: Paulist Press, 1979. Excellent on permission to express anger toward God.

Summary of Theological Responses to Suffering and Evil

Radical Solutions

1. *Limited God.* There is a perpetual struggle between ultimate powers, Good against Evil, and the power of Evil is the cause of the ills we suffer.
2. *Unjust God.* Evil is either permitted or willed by God, because God is indifferent or malicious toward us.
3. *Illusion.* The ills we seem to suffer are actually illusory, the result of erroneous thinking.
4. *Atheism.* The reality of evil in the world makes belief in God impossible.
5. *Mystery.* A problem that involves the power and purpose of the Infinite is beyond the capacity of finite minds to solve.

Solutions Redefining God's Omnipotence

6. *Freedom.* As finite creatures we are endowed by our Creator with freedom and, therefore, have the capacity to make bad or sinful choices, which result in evil consequences. *Subtypes:* (a) error, (b) sin, (c) fallenness, or original sin.
7. *Satan.* Within God's good creation there is a domain of evil powers (Satan and the demons), who are fallen from angelic status and insinuate evil into the world.
8. *Natural order.* Suffering is the unavoidable by-product of natural forces and rhythms operating in an ordered universe, which is itself God's good creation.
9. *Character development.* To achieve maturity, we must overcome hardship, anguish, and defeat.

Solutions Redefining God's Goodness

10. *Retribution.* Suffering is divine justice punishing our sinful ways.
11. *Testing.* Affliction is a God-given ordeal to put our faith to the test.